DINO COMPAGNI'S
CHRONICLE OF FLORENCE

University of Pennsylvania Press

MIDDLE AGES SERIES

Edited by

Edward Peters

Henry Charles Lea Professor

of Medieval History

University of Pennsylvania

A listing of the available books
in the series appears at the
back of this volume

DINO COMPAGNI'S
CHRONICLE OF FLORENCE

TRANSLATED, WITH AN INTRODUCTION AND NOTES,
BY DANIEL E. BORNSTEIN

 University of Pennsylvania Press · Philadelphia

Fourth paperback printing 1995

Printed in the United States of America

Library of Congress Cataloging-in-Publication Data
Compagni, Dino, 1260 (ca.)–1324.
  Dino Compagni's Chronicle of Florence.
  (The Middle Ages)
  Translation of: Cronica delle cose occorrenti ne'
tempi suoi.
  Includes index.
  1. Florence (Italy)—History—To 1421.   I. Title.
II. Title: Chronicle of Florence.   III. Series.
DG737.2.C73213   1986   945'.51   85-29517
ISBN 0-8122-8012-1 (alk. paper)
ISBN 0-8122-1221-5 (pbk.: alk. paper)

For Eric Cochrane
dedicated historian
and
buon cittadino popolano

CONTENTS

ACKNOWLEDGMENTS

I am grateful to Diane Owen Hughes for commenting on my introduction, and to Carol Lansing and several anonymous readers for scrutinizing both the introduction and the translation and suggesting a number of corrections and improvements. An appointment to the Michigan Society of Fellows gave me the free time to act on their suggestions. I also wish to thank my wife, Margery Schneider, for urging me to undertake this translation in the first place, and Edward Peters for recommending its inclusion in this series.

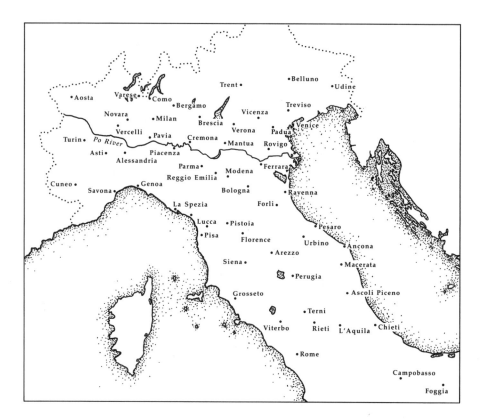

Northern and central Italy

INTRODUCTION

I

In 1300, Florence was at the height of its medieval glory. It was one of the largest cities in Europe, a great commercial metropolis and a remarkable cultural center. Giotto was revolutionizing the art of painting by using life-sized, volumetric human figures to evoke a whole new range of feeling and expression.[1] The poets of the *dolce stil nuovo* were working a similar transformation of the vernacular love lyric: Guido Cavalcanti turned his poems into vehicles for philosophical reflection, and in composing the *Vita Nuova*, Dante Alighieri arranged his lyrics into a complex narrative of the course of his love for Beatrice. The chroniclers Dino Compagni and Giovanni Villani recorded the daily life of their city in vibrant detail. These authors wrote in the knowledge that they had a cultivated and literate audience: Villani estimated that in the Florence of his day eight to ten thousand boys and girls were learning to read, another thousand to twelve hundred boys were continuing their education by studying the mathematics necessary to a business career, and 550 to 600 others were pursuing advanced studies in Latin and philosophy.[2] His chronicle was a great success with this audience, and was copied and recopied scores of times. Dino Compagni's chronicle, as we shall see, had quite a different fate.

Simply feeding the 100,000 people of Florence was a major undertaking. According to Giovanni Villani's description of Florence in the 1330s, every day the populace of Florence consumed over 2,000 bushels of grain; turning that grain into bread kept 146 bakeries busy. The Florentines washed that bread down with 70,000 quarts of wine a day. To provide their meat, about

---

1. John Larner, *Culture and Society in Italy 1290–1420* (London: B. T. Batsford, 1971), 9.
2. Giovanni Villani, *Cronica*, XI, 94.

4,000 cattle, 60,000 sheep, 20,000 goats, and 30,000 pigs were slaughtered every year.[3]

Housing this populace required an equally massive effort. The old city walls of 1172 enclosed only two hundred acres, and within that cramped space houses were densely packed. They typically rose five or six floors, with shops at street level and living quarters above. The houses of the great families of Florence were somewhat grander than these wooden tenements; their owners proclaimed their standing in the city by enlarging their palaces and erecting high towers (I, 20). As the population of Florence quadrupled in the course of the thirteenth century, thanks in large part to a massive influx of immigrants from the surrounding areas, the space within the walls quickly became inadequate and suburbs grew up beyond the city gates. At the end of the century work began on a new circuit of walls, some five miles in circumference, designed to enclose not only the built-up suburbs but also enough empty space to allow for future growth.[5]

These ambitious new walls were not the only great project which kept the carpenters and masons of Florence busy in the second half of the thirteenth century. As Richard Goldthwaite notes, this was a great period of church building:

> The Humiliati at Ognissanti, the Servites at the Santissima Annunziata, the Augustinians at Santo Spirito, the Carmelites at the church of the Carmine, and, largest of all, the Franciscans at Santa Croce and the Dominicans at Santa Maria Novella—all these establishments were rebuilt or built anew in the second half of the century.[6]

The reconstruction of the old Benedictine monastery of Santo Stefano began in 1294, at the same time as the new circuit of walls; the slow transformation of the cathedral church of Santa Reparata into the Duomo as it exists today began in 1296. Great civic monuments, too, rose in the thirteenth century. The Bargello, built to house the Captain of the Popolo, was completed

3. Ibid. On the economy of Florence, see Enrico Fiumi, *Fioritura e decadenza dell'economia fiorentina* (Florence: Olschki, 1977), and "La demografia fiorentina nelle pagine di Giovanni Villani," *Archivio Storico Italiano*, 108 (1950), 78–158.

4. The numbers in parentheses refer to the text of Dino Compagni's *Chronicle*: the roman numeral identifies the book and the arabic numeral the chapter. These divisions were introduced into the text by its modern editor, Isidoro Del Lungo; I have retained them because of their convenience.

5. On the growth of Florence in the thirteenth century, see Franek Sznura, *L'espansione urbana di Firenze nel Dugento* (Florence: La Nuova Italia, 1975).

6. Richard Goldthwaite, *The Building of Renaissance Florence* (Baltimore: Johns Hopkins University Press, 1980), 2.

in 1255; work on the Palace of the Priors (known today as the Palazzo Vecchio) began in 1299.

The third great industry of Florence was the production of woolen cloth. Thousands of workers were employed in washing, carding, and spinning the wool and in weaving, fulling, dyeing, shearing, and mending the cloth; hundreds more were involved in providing the wool workers with the supplies, tools, and buildings they needed. All told, according to Villani, about one-third of the populace earned its living from the three hundred or so workshops of the wool industry.[7] Hidetoshi Hoshino has recently questioned whether these shops actually produced the 100,000 pieces of cloth a year that Villani says they produced around 1300.[8] But even if Villani's figures are revised sharply downwards, as Hoshino says they must be, the weight of the wool industry in the Florentine economy was still considerable.

The cloth trade was international in scope, and, in contrast to construction and alimentation, it brought wealth into the city. The great merchants of the wool guild imported wool from England and exported finished cloth; the merchants of the Calimala guild imported rough cloth, finished it in Florence, and shipped it on to other markets. These men, together with the silk merchants and major retailers of the guild of Por Santa Maria and the bankers of the Cambio guild, made Florence an international economic power. The gold florin of Florence was the standard currency of the international trade; the Florentine bankers were the masters of international finance; the merchants of Florence were found everywhere that there was money to be made, leading Pope Boniface VIII to exclaim that the Florentines were the fifth element of the world. Boniface was in a position to know, for he himself depended on Florentine bankers such as the Spini to manage the papal finances and collect the papal revenues (I, 21). The great merchants of Florence, conscious of their wealth and confident of their power, hired the services of Charles of Valois, brother of the king of France; they summoned cardinals to do their bidding and sent them packing when they were no longer wanted. The Cardinal of Prato marveled at the arrogance of these

7. Villani, *Cronica*, XI, 94. For contrasting descriptions of the work force of Florence, see Raymond de Roover, "Labour Conditions in Florence around 1400: Theory, Policy and Reality," in *Florentine Studies: Politics and Society in Renaissance Florence*, ed. Nicolai Rubinstein (Evanston: Northwestern University Press, 1968), 277–313; and Victor Rutenburg, *Popolo e movimenti popolari nell'Italia del '300 e '400* (Bologna: Il Mulino, 1971), 25–88.

8. Hidetoshi Hoshino, *L'arte della lana in Firenze nel basso medioevo* (Florence: Olschki, 1980), 194ff.

Florentines, who thought that they could bribe any lord and manipulate any ruler (III, 32).

II

At the very height of its prosperity, this proud and confident community was torn by political turmoil and bitter factional strife.[9] According to Florentine tradition, the fundamental rift occurred in 1215, with the murder of Buondelmonte de' Buondelmonti. Of course, this was not the first instance of civil discord in Florence; however, it was from this time that, as Dino Compagni says, "the two factions called themselves enemies under two new names, that is, Guelf and Ghibelline" (I, 2). The adoption of these names and the larger political allegiances they signified meant that Florentine factional strife was no longer a purely local concern, circumscribed by the city walls. The Ghibelline party supported the claims of the Holy Roman Emperor to sovereignty over Italy; the Guelf party sided instead with the pope and with the French monarchy, rivals of the Hohenstaufen emperors. But in practice, the universal claims of pope and emperor were often of less immediate significance than were local interests and rivalries. Florence was only one of a number of city–states in central Italy; as it expanded, it came into conflict with its Tuscan neighbors: Pisa, Siena, Arezzo, Lucca, and Pistoia.[10] Each city aligned itself with the Guelf or Ghibelline cause according to the affiliations of its nearest and most dangerous rivals: if Lucca was Guelf, Pisa was Ghibelline; if Florence was Guelf, Arezzo was Ghibelline; and so on. Each Guelf city tried to subvert its Ghibelline neighbors by backing their internal Guelf factions, as (for instance) the Florentine Guelfs incited the Guelfs of Arezzo to seize power from the Ghibelline rulers of that city (I, 6). When the losers in these local power struggles fled or were exiled from their native

9. The classic interpretations of Florentine politics at the end of the thirteenth century are those of Gaetano Salvemini, *Magnati e popolani in Firenze dal 1280 al 1295* (Florence, 1899; reprint Milan: Feltrinelli, 1960), and Nicola Ottokar, *Il Comune di Firenze alla fine del Dugento* (Florence, 1926; reprint Turin: Einaudi, 1962). A major recent study is that of Sergio Raveggi, Massimo Tarassi, Daniela Medici, and Patrizia Parenti, *Ghibellini, Guelfi e Popolo Grasso: I detentori del potere politico a Firenze nella seconda metà del Dugento* (Florence: La Nuova Italia, 1978). I have also benefited from Carol Leroy Lansing, "Nobility in a Medieval Commune: The Florentine Magnates, 1260–1300" (Ph.D. diss. University of Michigan, 1984), which Professor Lansing kindly made available to me.

10. For two good general studies of the city–states of medieval Italy, see J. K. Hyde, *Society and Politics in Medieval Italy* (London: Macmillan, 1973), and Daniel Waley, *The Italian City–Republics* (New York: McGraw–Hill, 1969).

cities, they could count on finding refuge and support in a neighboring city, as the Aretine Guelfs did in Florence when their attempted coup failed.[11] And so the factional strife of each city became entangled in a network of regional politics and international allegiances, as that of Florence did when Buondelmonte was murdered at the instigation of the Uberti—a family with imperial sympathies.

The political life of Florence was further complicated by the efforts of new persons and groups to win a share of power. Throughout the twelfth century, a small group of patrician families had been the unquestioned masters of the city. The members of this patriciate generally combined urban and rural interests: they owned land in the *contado*, that rural area immediately surrounding Florence and subject to the city, and they invested in moneychanging and commerce. These men served as consuls, filled the town councils, and formed the core of the town militia; indeed, because they fought in the militia as mounted knights and so had titles to buttress the antiquity of their lineages, they came to be identified as the nobility of Florence.[12] However, the demographic explosion and commercial expansion of the thirteenth century brought new contenders for power. The immigrants who swelled the population of Florence were often persons of substance; they owned rural estates or had professional training as lawyers or notaries.[13] Once established in Florence, they became involved in commerce; and they, like other non–noble merchants, professionals, and landowners, prospered in the favorable economic climate. These prosperous newcomers to the patriciate rivaled the old consular nobility in wealth and imitated it in their manner of life; some of them, indeed, merged with it. But others remained identified as the *popolo*, the "people," in distinction from the nobles or magnates, and vied with them for political power. The *popolo*, however, was not a homogeneous group; it included both the *popolani grassi*, the wealthy non-nobles who matched the magnates in wealth and ostentation and sought to match them in political power, and the *popolo minuto*, the more modest merchants, shopkeepers, and artisans who could only hope to share in political power through their participation in such corporate groups as the guilds and the militia companies. It did not include the thousands of ordinary la-

11. On the communities of exiles which dotted medieval Italy and helped keep it in turmoil, see Randolph Starn, *Contrary Commonwealth: The Theme of Exile in Medieval and Renaissance Italy* (Berkeley: University of California Press, 1982).

12. See Gaetano Salvemini, *La dignità cavalleresca nel comune di Firenze* (Florence, 1896; reprint Milan: Feltrinelli, 1972).

13. Johan Plesner, *L'émigration de la campagne à la ville libre de Florence au XIIIe siècle* (Copenhagen, 1934).

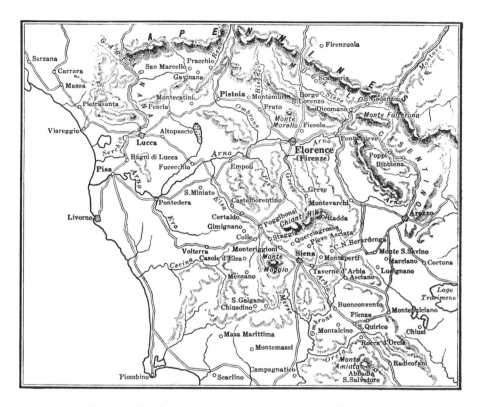

Tuscany (from Ferdinand Schevill, Medieval and Renaissance Florence *[New York: Harper & Row, 1963], vol. 1, opp. p. 74)*

borers in the wool industry and construction trades, who remained excluded from direct participation in Florentine politics.

Florentine political life, with its complex fractures and its intricate ties to foreign powers, was volatile and often violent. Triumphs or defeats on distant battlefields could bring about sudden changes in Florence. Emperor Frederick II crushed his enemies at Cortenuova late in 1237, and the following year, in the flush of victory, he claimed the right of confirming the podestà of Florence. The podestà was the chief executive of the city government; to ensure his neutrality and independence, the podestà was not a citizen of Florence, and to ensure his honesty, he was subjected to an audit at the end of his year in office. By controlling the selection of the podestà, Frederick II was transforming this official, who was supposed to be a neutral restraint on factional strife, into a partisan of the Ghibelline faction. When he went so far as to appoint his illegitimate son Frederick of Antioch to the

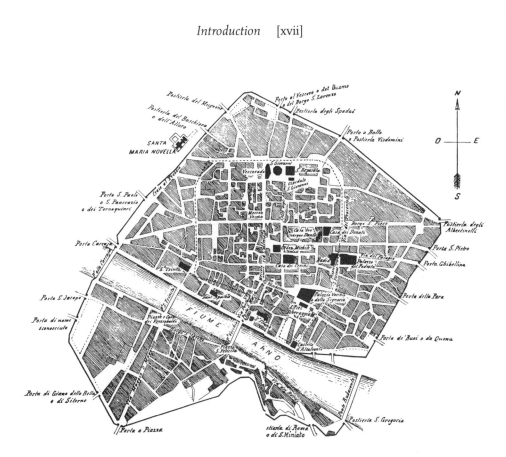

Florence in the early fourteenth century (from Dino Compagni, Cronica *[Torino: Einaudi, 1968])*

post in 1246, the result was open violence and, in 1248, the exile of the Guelfs from Florence.

This Ghibelline triumph proved fleeting. At the close of the year 1250, the Florentine Ghibellines suffered a double disaster: they were defeated in battle by the Guelf exiles, and their protector Frederick II died. The result was a revolt in Florence and the establishment of the Primo Popolo. This regime preserved the traditional organs of government but added a second, parallel series of institutions intended to represent the interests of the *popolo,* just as the podestà and his councils represented the noble lineages. A military organization of neighborhood companies was established, a Captain of the Popolo was named, and two advisory councils were formed, one representing the six administrative districts into which the city was divided and the other representing the greater guilds.

In 1260, the imperial cause was again in the ascendent, under the leadership of Frederick's son Manfred. The Ghibelline exiles and their Sienese allies defeated the Florentine Guelfs in the battle of Montaperti. The Primo Popolo collapsed as the Guelf patricians fled the city, and the old system of government by Ghibelline podestà was reestablished. This regime fell in its turn with the defeat of Manfred by the Guelf champion, Charles of Anjou, in 1266. After a short-lived experiment in popular government, the Guelf patricians, with the backing of Angevin troops, assumed control of the city. They abolished the office of Captain of the Popolo and formalized the position of the Guelf Party in the city: in addition to administering the goods confiscated from the Ghibelline exiles, the Party was given the right of scrutinizing all persons chosen for public office, to ensure that no Ghibellines or Ghibelline sympathizers had access to political power. From this point on, Florence was firmly Guelf and usually allied with the papacy and with the Angevin rulers of the Kingdom of Naples.

Unfortunately for Florence, its papal and Angevin allies did not always see eye to eye. The fear of any one ruler becoming too powerful in Italy had inspired the popes throughout their long struggle against the Holy Roman Emperors; now that the Ghibellines had been decisively defeated and the Hohenstaufen dynasty had died out, the pope's Angevin allies seemed dangerously strong. To balance the power of Charles of Anjou, popes Gregory X (1271–1276) and Nicholas III (1277–1280) tried to revive their former foes, the Ghibellines. Nicholas sent a legate to Florence to arrange a reconciliation between the Guelfs and the Ghibellines, and in 1280 the papal legate, Cardinal Latino, summoned home those Ghibellines who had not attempted to return to Florence by force of arms. He then established a government in which power was shared between the Guelfs and the repatriated Ghibellines (I, 3). But peace proved fleeting; "the Guelfs, who were more powerful, began gradually to contravene the peace pacts" (I, 4), and they quickly stripped the Ghibellines of their rights. Then, in 1282, the revolt known as the Sicilian Vespers shook Angevin power in Italy, the hold of the Guelf nobles was loosened, and for the second time the *popolo* won a share of power in Florence.[14]

The council of fourteen which had headed the regime of 1280 was gradually replaced by the Priors of the Guilds (I, 4). Initially only three Priors were chosen, but their number was soon increased to six, one from each sixth of the city. To prevent excessive concentration of power in the hands of any one person, the Priors' term in office was a mere two months, and they

14. On the international repercussions of the Sicilian Vespers, see Steven Runciman, *The Sicilian Vespers* (Cambridge: Cambridge University Press, 1958).

were forbidden to hold office again for two or (after 1290) three years. At first, the only people eligible to serve as Priors were the members of the greater guilds: the cloth importers and finishers of the Calimala guild, the moneychangers of the Cambio guild, the silk merchants and leading retailers of the guild of Por Santa Maria, the wool manufacturers, the lawyers and notaries, and the doctors and apothecaries—in short, the mercantile and professional elite. In 1287, access to the priorate was opened to the five middle guilds (the butchers, shoemakers, blacksmiths, master builders, and used cloth dealers), and in the 1290s, eligibility was granted to the nine minor guilds (the wine retailers, innkeepers, sellers of oil and cheese, tanners, armorers, ironworkers, girdlemakers, and bakers).[15] These 21 guilds with rights to office did not exhaust the number of trade associations in Florence: Dino Compagni refers to 72 guilds which had their own consuls (II, 7). But they did include many of the more important groups involved in the construction trades and in alimentation, who thus came to share the right to hold office along with the merchant, banking, and professional elite.

The priorate was intended to institutionalize the interests of the *popolo*. However, the *popolo* included men of widely varying status, and it was the richest and most prominent among them—the *popolani grassi*—who tended to be chosen Priors. Since the *popolani grassi* were linked to the Guelf magnates by commercial interests and by kinship, the office which had been created to protect the *popolo* soon came to serve the patriciate. And so, Dino noted, "for these reasons the good *popolani* citizens were unhappy, and they blamed the office of the Priors, because the Guelf magnates had become lords" (I, 5).

After a decade of domination by the Guelf magnates, the *popolo* found a champion in Giano della Bella. Under his leadership, the Ordinances of Justice were passed in 1293: the magnates were required to post surety for their good behavior, they were held liable for crimes committed by their kinsmen, and they were barred from holding the highest offices in the city government. To enforce these laws, the office of Standard-bearer of Justice was created, and the holder of this office (who, like the Priors, served a two–month term) was provided with a thousand armed men (I, 11). With this institutional innovation, the government of Florence assumed the shape it was to maintain until the fall of the republic.

Despite the Ordinances of Justice, the magnates retained a great deal of

15. On these constitutional developments, see John M. Najemy, *Corporatism and Consensus in Florentine Electoral Politics 1280–1400* (Chapel Hill: University of North Carolina Press, 1982).

power thanks to their wealth, their numbers, their prestige, and their experience in arms and diplomacy; and in 1295 they engineered the expulsion of Giano della Bella from Florence. Then the magnates, politically dominant despite being officially disenfranchised, split into two factions: the Black Guelfs, led by Corso Donati, and the White Guelfs, headed by Vieri de' Cerchi. The story of this rift and the subsequent defeat of the Whites in 1301 provided the bitter core of Dino Compagni's chronicle. But not its end: the victorious Blacks split in turn as Corso Donati fell out with four other leaders of the faction—Rosso della Tosa, Pazzino de' Pazzi, Betto Brunelleschi, and Geri Spini—and was defeated by them.

III

As Dino Compagni says (I, 1), no one was better placed than he to describe the factional conflicts of those years.[16] He was a successful merchant, inscribed in the guild of Por Santa Maria. His repeated election as one of the four consuls of his guild attests to his prominence: he served six-month terms as consul in 1282, 1286, 1289, 1291, 1294, and 1299. He was also a member of the important confraternity of the Madonna of Or San Michele, which was founded in 1291 to foster the cult of that miracle-working image (III, 8), and in 1298 he held the office of captain of the confraternity.

Compagni's political career was equally respectable. In 1282, he and five other *popolani* citizens played a leading role in the establishment of the Priors of the Guilds (I, 4). He himself served as one of the Priors from April 15 to June 15, 1289; during his term in office, the Florentines defeated Arezzo in the battle of Campaldino. Four years later, from June 15 to August 15, 1293, he served as Standard-bearer of Justice, the third person to hold that recently instituted office and so one of the first to put into effect the harsh penalties decreed by the Ordinances of Justice (I, 12). Throughout this period, during which Giano della Bella dominated the political life of Florence, Dino's advice was regularly sought by the Priors and by the town councils; in December, 1294, he and Giano were part of the commission of fourteen citizens charged with reforming the statutes (I, 13–14). But when Giano was exiled on March 5, 1295, the political career of his follower, Dino, also suffered: for the next five years Dino held no public office, nor was his

16. The following summary of Compagni's career is based on the entry by Girolamo Arnaldi in the *Dizionario Biografico degli Italiani*, 27 (1982), 629–647, and on Arnaldi's expanded version of that entry, "Dino Compagni cronista e militante 'popolano,'" *La Cultura*, 21 (1983), 37–82.

opinion sought by those who did. When he returned to public prominence in 1300, he dedicated himself to the thankless task of maintaining concord in the increasingly polarized city. He was one of the counselors who advised the Priors to banish the leaders of both the Cerchi and Donati factions after the disorders on St. John's Eve in 1300 (I, 21). When some members of the Donati faction were discovered plotting against the government, he tried to reconcile the conspirators with the Priors (I, 24). He himself was once more one of the Priors in October, 1301, when Charles of Valois was approaching Florence and the conflict between the Blacks and the Whites neared its climax. He described himself and his fellow Priors as good, peaceloving men and supporters of unity—but also as fatally weak (II, 5). Rather than taking forceful action, they merely asked the leaders of the factions to swear an oath of concord (II, 8), and when this did nothing to restrain the Blacks, Dino and the other Priors watched helplessly as the city slipped from their control. They were forced to resign their offices on November 8, having served less than half of their terms (II, 15–21).

Dino Compagni thus participated directly in several key events in the political life of Florence: the establishment of the priorate, the application of the Ordinances of Justice, the revision of the statutes, and the final collapse of the White party in Florence. He knew at first hand the failure of the commune to restrain the fomenters of factional violence and the futility of all efforts at reconciliation. He earned the knowledge and wisdom which is condensed in the pages of his chronicle through bitter experience.

The political career which brought him this experience was respectable, but not extraordinary. The Florentine political system, with its short terms in office followed by long intervals of ineligibility, made it difficult for any one figure to be truly preeminent in civic life, and only Giano della Bella and Corso Donati ever achieved that sort of commanding position in Dino's lifetime. Dino's career was notable less for its success than for its independence. He was the only member of his family to hold public office in the last two decades of the thirteenth century.[17] Most public figures of this period came from powerful families and could rely on the support of their relatives; Dino's success without the aid of office-holding kinsmen is a good indication of his personal abilities. Nor were his relatives by marriage any help: indeed, they were generally of the opposite party. His first wife, Filippa, received a bequest from Andrea da Cerreto, that "wise jurist from an old Ghibelline family who had become a Black Guelf" (II, 10). Andrea da

17. His brother Guido was elected only once, in 1297, to the position of consul of the guild of Por Santa Maria, an office which Dino held six times.

Cerreto was one of the Priors who replaced Dino and his fellows in November 1301 and winked at the pillaging of Florence (II, 19).[18] His second wife, Francesca, was from a family of Black Guelfs; her brother, Vanni, was prominent in that party and became Prior nine times. His youngest son, Bartolomeo, married a daughter of Pazzino de' Pazzi, one of the leaders of the Black Guelfs. But despite all of these marriage ties to the Blacks, Dino himself sided with the White Guelfs. Nor were these ties of any help to Dino when his Whites were defeated. "Kinship and friendship were worth nothing," said Dino of the convulsive moment of defeat; "new marriages were worth nothing; every friend became an enemy; brother abandoned brother, son abandoned father" (II, 23). He was saved from exile not by any personal connections, but by a law which protected the former Priors from judicial proceedings for a year after leaving office. But the defeat of his party meant that Dino's public career was ended: he never again held public office, nor guild office, nor even office in his confraternity. He lived the rest of his life, until his death in 1324, like an exile in his own city, tending quietly to his modest business and mulling over the events which had led to his party's defeat.

IV

The fruit of Dino's reflection is the chronicle translated here.[19] It was not written as an immediate record of events; as Dino says in the prologue, he put off writing for many years. His claim that he felt inadequate to the task, however, is a rhetorical commonplace, and it is easy to see far more cogent reasons for his delay. The Florence of 1302 simply had no audience for such a work: the victorious Blacks would not have welcomed his fierce denunciation of their arrogance and cruelty, and the defeated Whites would hardly have been any more receptive to his bitter dissection of their weakness and

18. See also Dino's harsh words about him in II, 29.

19. The fundamental edition of the chronicle is that by Isidoro Del Lungo, *Dino Compagni e la sua Cronica* (Florence: Le Monnier, 1878–1887). Del Lungo published a revised edition of the text in the *Rerum Italicarum Scriptores*, new ed., vol. IX, part 2 (Città di Castello: S. Lapi, 1913), 1–266. This revised edition was reprinted recently with introduction and notes by Gino Luzzatto: Dino Compagni, *Cronica* (Turin: Einaudi, 1968). In preparing my translation, I have relied on Del Lungo's massive commentary and notes and on Luzzatto's notes.

This chronicle was not Dino's only literary effort. As a young man, he had tried his hand at lyric poetry; a handful of his rather mediocre sonnets and one moral *canzone* have survived. In addition, an allegorical poem of some three hundred lines known as the *Intelligenza* has been attributed to him by some critics.

vacillation. The situation was different in 1310. Henry of Luxembourg had been elected Holy Roman Emperor, and in October 1310 he crossed the Alps into Italy. The vision of Henry on his journey south, "passing from city to city, making peace as if he were an angel of God" (III, 24), stirred the hopes of the White Guelfs in general and of Dino Compagni in particular. Suddenly it seemed likely that the political situation of Florence would change, that his party would return to power, and that there would be an audience for what Dino had to say. And so, at a distance of nearly three decades from the institution of the priorate in 1282 and of ten years from the crucial events of 1300–1301 which form the core of the chronicle (I, 21–II, 24), he began to set his reflections down in writing.

The lapse of time between the events and Dino's account of them encouraged a number of minor inaccuracies. Whether from lack of interest or lack of information, Dino provided very few precise dates, and several of those which he did provide were incorrect. He could not remember some details, such as the exact number of families declared to be magnates in 1293 (I, 11), the date on which the Black Guelfs took arms to seize the city (II, 15), and the date of Corso Donati's death (III, 21). He recalled other details incorrectly, as when he identified the bishop of Arezzo as one of the Pazzi rather than one of the Ubertini (I, 6), when he attributed the initial redaction of the Ordinances of Justice to Giano della Bella (I, 11), and when he claimed to have been the first Standard-bearer of Justice to destroy the houses of a magnate in accordance with the Ordinances of Justice (I, 12). Some of these errors may involve more than simple lapses of memory, for Dino may at times have distorted his account to magnify his own importance or that of his hero, Giano della Bella.[20]

But these occasional inaccuracies of detail are outweighed by the coherence of vision, the awareness of the overall pattern of events, and the focus on the essential which the passage of time also brought. Freed from the constraints of chronicling events as they occurred, Dino wrote to elucidate a single topic. All else was ignored; Dino's chronicle has none of the wonderful profusion of variegated detail which makes Giovanni Villani's chronicle (written just a few years later) such a rich source of information on so many aspects of Florentine life. Instead, Dino's offers dramatic unity, an impassioned concentration of attention, and an unsparing examination of a single aspect of Florentine life: the factional strife which convulsed the city at the end of the thirteenth century.

20. It is noteworthy that Dino makes just one passing reference to the person who is today the best known of his contemporaries: Dante Alighieri.

Dino saw the course of Florentine history as a series of fractures: each time order was established in the city, the ruling group broke into two factions, one of which triumphed over the other and then split in its turn. He reported only a single event from before his own lifetime—the murder of Buondelmonte—and although he apologized for recounting this bit of ancient history, he had a good reason for including it: "to open the way to an understanding of how the accursed parties of the Guelfs and Ghibellines were formed in Florence" (I, 2). The rest of his chronicle was concerned with events of his adulthood, starting with the precarious equilibrium established by Cardinal Latino in 1280. From that moment, fracture succeeded fracture in rapid succession. The Guelfs exiled the Ghibellines and then split into the partisans and opponents of Giano della Bella. His magnate foes exiled Giano and then split into Blacks and Whites. The Blacks exiled the Whites and then split into factions headed by Corso Donati and Rosso della Tosa. And so it went, in a dizzying and increasingly violent series of fractures within the ruling group.

These fractures occurred with such inexorable regularity that they might have seemed natural, inevitable features of Florentine life. But Dino recognized that these fractures did not follow the divisions of Florentine society; they cut across those divisions, and even the most seemingly "natural" of bonds, that of kinship, did not always hold people together, as close relatives aligned themselves with opposing factions. Nor did he conceive of Florentine society itself as divided into natural categories; these categories were culturally defined, like the magnates, "who were not all noble by blood, but for other reasons were labeled magnates" (I, 13). The factions, too, were artificial constructs, formed by people who came together for a variety of reasons: personal sympathy, financial obligation, business partnership, kinship, resentment of and rivalry with members of the opposing party, and more. Consider the diversity of bonds that went into the formation of the Cerchi and Donati factions (I, 22):

All the Ghibellines sided with the Cerchi because they hoped to receive less harm from them, and so did all those who had been of Giano della Bella's mind, since the Cerchi had appeared to mourn his exile. Also of their party were Guido di messer Cavalcante Cavalcanti, because he was an enemy of messer Corso Donati; Naldo Gherardini, because he was an enemy of the Manieri, relatives of messer Corso; messer Manetto Scali and his family, because they were relatives of the Cerchi; messer Lapo Salterelli, their kinsman; messer Berto Frescobaldi, because he had received large loans from them; messer Goccia Adimari, because he was their business associate; messer Biligiardo, Baschiera, and Baldo della Tosa, out of dislike for their kinsman messer Rosso, because thanks to him they had been deprived of their honors. The Mozzi, the main branch of the Cavalcanti, and many other great families and *popolani* sided with them.

With the party of messer Corso Donati sided messer Rosso, messer Arrigo, messer Nepo, and Pinuccio della Tosa, out of long familiarity and friendship; messer Gherardo Ventraia, messer Geri Spini and his relatives, because they had offended the Cerchi; messer Gherardo Sgrana and messer Bindello, out of familiarity and friendship; messer Pazzino de' Pazzi and his relatives, the Rossi, most of the Bardi, the Bordoni, the Cerretani, Borgo Rinaldi, Manzuolo, the Sheep the butcher, and many others.

These complex factions with their diversity of interests did not come together naturally. They had to be deliberately assembled, and the means used to assemble them were as diverse as the bonds which united them. When the Black Guelfs split after their victory over the Whites, Rosso della Tosa attracted his followers through calculated magnanimity, loaning money without expecting to be repaid and making peace with people who had offended him. Corso Donati, in contrast, used his eloquence to win the backing of all those with grudges against the ruling group: the magnates, who thought that they had been deprived of their due; the common people, who suspected the rulers of manipulating grain prices in a time of scarcity; even some relatives of messer Rosso,[21] who had fallen out with their kinsman over a property dispute (III, 2; see also III, 19).

The impulse which brought these complex groups into conflict was, in contrast, quite simple: competition for office. Office-holding meant prestige, profit, and, above all, power. It meant having an armed retinue, apportioning taxes, setting grain prices, and authorizing expenditures. It meant receiving requests, making decisions, and granting favors (see III, 19). It also meant being able to manipulate the judicial institutions of the city, to speed legal proceedings against foes or rivals and to deflect or delay them when they threatened friends (III, 37).

The ease with which public office could be turned to private ends explains the ferocity with which people competed for it and the futility of Dino Compagni's oft-advanced solution to that competition: an equitable division of the offices. Dino approved of Cardinal Latino's attempted solution in 1280, but since the council of fourteen created by the cardinal included eight Guelfs and only six Ghibellines, the Guelfs controlled the government and soon stripped the Ghibellines of their share (I, 3). After 1293 no even divi-

21. "Messer" was the title given to knights and lawyers; "ser" was the title given to notaries.

sion of offices was possible, for the *signoria* was made up of an odd number of officials: the six Priors and the Standard-bearer of Justice. In 1301, when Dino confronted the intractable problem of sharing an odd number of offices evenly between the two factions, he and his fellow Priors tried to solve this problem by allotting three offices to each faction. "As for the seventh, since it could not be split, we chose someone of so little value that no one feared him" (II, 12). In doing so, they acknowledged that a mechanical division of the offices into two equal portions, even if it had been possible, would not have solved the problem. After all, the value of the offices depended on the vigor of the persons who occupied them. Rosso della Tosa and his partisans recognized this when they sought to exclude Corso Donati from any share of office: "They feared his proud spirit and energy, and did not believe that he could be satisfied with a share of power" (III, 19). And so all attempts to achieve a solution by sharing the offices foundered on the practical difficulty of creating a perfectly equal balance of forces—and maintaining that balance every time a new *signoria* was chosen, six times a year.

Attempted solutions also foundered on the passions of the men involved. Dino Compagni had a sense of the devastating power of passion that went beyond the driving self–interest of a Corso Donati or a Rosso della Tosa. He perceived that the burning passions of these men often led them into behavior which meant the destruction of themselves and of everyone around them.

For Dino, "burning passion" was not a trite metaphor; he saw the unrestrained drive for power as frankly incendiary, and so described it in a vocabulary of heat and flames. Giano della Bella's enemies tried to get him in trouble by setting him "ablaze about justice" (I, 13). Corso Donati fanned his faction's resentment of Rosso della Tosa's power, and "the fire grew so hot" that some of Corso's followers tried to kill one of Rosso's (III, 19). The reaction of Rosso and his partisans was to become "so inflamed with talk that they could not hold back from havoc" (III, 20). But the passage in which passion, fire, and destruction are most tightly bound together is III, 8. After the cardinal of Prato had been frightened into leaving Florence, "spirits grew so heated (*tanto s'accesono gli animi*) that people took arms and began to harm one another." And their weapon of choice was fire, as the metaphorical flames of passion lit a real fire which gutted the center of Florence. The physical and moral devastation left by this fire was the inescapable proof that burning passions had triumphed over the feeble good intentions of the peacemakers.

Yet Dino did not limit himself to a bleak Yeatsian judgment that the best lack all conviction while the worst are full of passionate intensity. He saw the fomenters of discord as doing something more serious than simply committing villainies against their fellow men; by harming the sacred community of Florence, they were sinning against God. Dino revealed his sense of the sacredness of Florence by taking recourse to religious actions—to oaths and processions—in the effort to quell factional violence (II, 8 and 13), and by using a religious vocabulary to describe the honest performance of the duties of political office. When the Priors went to dine with Charles of Valois, putting themselves in the hands of that treacherous lord, "many citizens mourned for us at that excursion, thinking that those who went were going to their martyrdom" (II, 13). And when Noffo Guidi asked Dino to betray the White Guelfs and give the Blacks a majority in the *signoria*, Dino replied that that would make him a Judas, and that he would feed his children to the dogs before he committed such treason (II, 12). But despite Dino's bold statement, the leaders of the Blacks took arms, threw Florence into anarchy, and mercilessly pillaged and oppressed their adversaries.

Dino perceived two sorts of divine retribution for these sins against Florence. The hand of God executed justice on individual evildoers: some of them died in particularly painful or humiliating circumstances (III, 38–40), and five of the leading instigators of factional violence even happened to be killed in the plot of land where criminals were executed (III, 41). But divine justice was also at work in a more general way, by leading Henry of Luxembourg to Italy to punish the entire city of Florence. When Dino wrote the final words of his chronicle, Henry was about to attack Florence; the vengeance of God was at hand (III, 42). Here was the true peacemaker who would undo the work of that false peacemaker, Charles of Valois; here was the angel of God who would put an end to the long sequence of fractures and factions and restore order to Florence.

V

Dino's hopes proved illusory. Henry died; the Blacks consolidated their hold on Florence; and Dino's chronicle had to be hidden away. For three centuries it was nearly unknown; only two copies of it were made, one sometime late in the fifteenth century and the other in 1514. It was not until the seventeenth century that the chronicle began to attract interest as an example of Tuscan prose from the time of Dante and manuscripts of it began to circulate; it was published for the first time in 1726, more than four hundred years after it was written. It then began to receive extravagant praise: Dino was called a new Sallust, a Caesar, a Tacitus, an Italian Herodotus or

Thucydides; he was paired with his fellow White Guelf, Dante Alighieri, and the period around 1300 was referred to as the age of Dino and Dante. This puffery provoked a critical reaction; late in the nineteenth century several scholars went so far as to argue that the chronicle was a forgery.[22] But those arguments were rebutted at the turn of the century by Isidoro Del Lungo, who in the course of defending the authenticity of Dino's chronicle provided the historical commentary needed to understand this densely packed and occasionally elliptical text. Thanks largely to his efforts, it is now possible to leave behind the excessive adulation and skepticism of the last century and see Dino's chronicle for what it is: a vivid description and acute analysis of the political life of one of the greatest of medieval cities.

22. For a summary of the critical fortunes of Compagni's chronicle, see Arnaldi's entry in the *Dizionario Biografico degli Italiani* (cited above, note 16), 640ff. Arnaldi also provides, on pp. 646–47, a bibliography of the literature on the chronicle. In exploring that literature, a good starting point is Raffaello Morghen, "La storiografia fiorentina del Trecento: Ricordano Malispini, Dino Compagni, e Giovanni Villani," in his *Civiltà medioevale al tramonto* (Bari: Laterza, 1973).

DINO COMPAGNI'S
CHRONICLE OF FLORENCE

PROLOGUE

For a long time the memory of the ancient histories has spurred me to write of the perilous and unfortunate events which this noble city, daughter of Rome, has borne for many years and especially in the time of the jubilee of 1300.[1] Excusing myself on the grounds that I was not sufficiently able and believing that someone else would write, I put off writing for a number of years. But since these perils and noteworthy events have so multiplied that they can no longer be left in silence, I now intend to write for the benefit of those who will inherit more fortunate times, so that they may recognize the gifts of God, who rules and governs through all times.

---

1. Giovanni Villani pays a similar tribute to the inspiration of the ancient historians of Rome, an inspiration which he says he felt when he made the jubilee pilgrimage to Rome in 1300. However, the authors he lists as "masters of history" include not just those we would classify as historians, such as Sallust and Livy, but poets like Virgil and Lucan. Giovanni Villani, *Cronica*, VIII, 37.

BOOK I

1 When I began, I intended to write the truth about certain things which I saw and heard, since they were notable events and no one truly saw them in their origins as I did. Those things which I did not see directly, I intended to write down as they were reported; and since many people, following their twisted desires, distort what they say and corrupt the truth, my intention was to write according to the best report. And so that foreigners may better understand the events which took place, let me describe the form of that noble city in the province of Tuscany, built under the sign of Mars, rich and ample with a regal river of fresh water which divides the city almost in half, temperate in climate, sheltered from harmful winds, poor in land, abundant with good products, its citizens bold in arms, proud and combative, and rich with unlawful profits, distrusted and feared for its greatness by the nearby cities, rather than loved.

Pisa is forty miles from Florence, Lucca is forty miles, Pistoia twenty miles, Bologna fifty-eight miles, Arezzo forty miles, and Siena thirty miles. San Miniato is twenty miles in the direction of Pisa, Prato is ten miles in the direction of Pistoia, Monte Accenico is twenty-two miles in the direction of Bologna, Figline is sixteen miles in the direction of Arezzo, Poggibonsi is sixteen miles in the direction of Siena. All of these cities possess many other villages and walled towns. And on all sides there are many noblemen, counts and captains, who love the city more in times of discord than in peacetime, and obey it more from fear than love. This city of Florence is very populous and its good climate promotes fecundity. Its citizens are well-bred and its women lovely and adorned; its buildings are beautiful and filled with many useful crafts, more than any other city in Italy. For these reasons many people from distant lands come to see Florence—not because they have to, but because of its crafts and guilds, and the beauty and decoration of the city.

2   May its citizens then weep for themselves and for their children, since by their pride and ill will and competition for office they have undone so noble a city, and abused its laws, and sold off in a moment the honors which their ancestors had acquired with great effort over many years. And may they look for God's justice, which by many signs promises to visit upon them the evil which is the guilty's due, for they were free and need not have been subjugated.

After many ancient evils resulting from the strife of its citizens, there arose in this city a new evil which divided all of its citizens in such a way that the two factions called themselves enemies under two new names, that is, Guelf and Ghibelline. And in Florence the cause of this was that a young nobleman of the city named Buondelmonte de' Buondelmonti had promised to take as his wife a daughter of messer Oderigo Giantruffetti.[1] Then one day, as he was passing by the house of the Donati, a gentlewoman named madonna Aldruda, wife of messer Forteguerra Donati, who had two lovely daughters, saw him from the balcony of her palace and called to him, and showed him one of her daughters, and said to him: "Who have you chosen to be your wife? I was saving this girl for you." He looked at the girl and was pleased by what he saw, but replied: "I cannot do anything about it now." At which madonna Aldruda said: "Of course you can, since I will pay the penalty for you." Buondelmonte replied: "And I do want her." And so he took her to be his wife, leaving the one he had chosen and to whom he was pledged. Messer Oderigo grieved over this with his relatives and friends, and they decided to avenge themselves, to strike down Buondelmonte and shame him. When the Uberti, a very noble and powerful family and relatives of Oderigo, heard this, they said that they would rather see him dead: the hatred provoked by a killing is no greater than that provoked by a few wounds; what's done is done.[2] They arranged to murder him on the day he married the woman; and so they did. As a result of this death the citizens became divided, and relatives and allies were drawn in on both sides so that there was no end to this rift, from which many fights and murders and civil

1. The other chroniclers say, however, that she was the daughter of Lambertuccio degli Amidei.
2. This famous phrase, "cosa fatta capo ha," is attributed by Dante to Mosca Lamberti. *Inferno*, XXVIII, 106–108.

battles were born. But since it is not my intention to write of things long past,[3] because sometimes the truth of them cannot be determined, I will let this drop. I have begun in this manner only to open the way to an understanding of how the accursed parties of the Guelfs and Ghibellines were formed in Florence: we will now return to the events of our times.

3   In the year of Christ's incarnation 1280, while the Guelf party held sway in Florence, the Ghibellines having been driven out, from a small spring welled a great river: that is, from a small disagreement in the Guelf party came a great agreement with the Ghibelline party. The Guelfs had become suspicious of one another and in their meetings and councils each one deprecated the words of the others, and the wisest among them were afraid of what might happen and saw indications of the results they feared: a noble Guelf citizen and knight named messer Buonaccorso degli Adimari, powerful because of his family and rich in possessions, grew so proud along with the other magnates that, paying no heed to the censures of his party, he married his son, messer Forese, to a daughter of the head of the Ghibelline party, Count Guido Novello of the house of the Counts Guidi. For these reasons the Guelfs, after many meetings at the Guelf Palace, decided to make peace with the exiled Ghibellines. They wisely decided to arrange peace with them under the yoke of the Church, so that the ties might be sustained by the strength of the Church; and they quietly arranged that the pope act as mediator to their discord. At their request he sent the friar and cardinal messer Latino to Florence to bring about peace between the two parties. When the cardinal arrived, he asked each side to select representatives who would give him power of arbitration; and they did so. On the strength of this agreement he declared that the Ghibellines could return to Florence, with many conditions and obligations, and he apportioned among them the offices of the surrounding areas; and for the government of the city he ordained fourteen citizens, eight Guelfs and six Ghibellines; and he set in order many other things, with penalties fixed for both parties, binding them under the Church of Rome. He had these laws and pacts and promises written down among the municipal laws of the city.

He ordered that the proud and powerful family of the Uberti remain in exile for a while, along with others of their party, though wherever they were they might enjoy their family possessions like the rest. And those who had to bear the burden of exile received from the Commune a daily stipend

---

3. The events he has been describing took place in 1215.

for their support, though those who were not knighted received less than the knights.

4 With both parties in the city and enjoying the benefits of the peace, the Guelfs, who were more powerful, began gradually to contravene the peace pacts. First they took the stipends away from the exiles; then they filled the offices irregularly; they declared the exiles to be rebels. Their overbearing behavior grew to the point that they stripped all the public offices and benefits from the Ghibellines, and discord grew between them. Some men, thinking of what might come from all this, sought out some leaders of the *popolo* to ask them to try to find a remedy, so that this discord would not destroy the city. Some of the popular party appreciated the value in what was said to them, and because of this six *popolani* citizens got together. I, Dino Compagni, was one of them: because of my youth I paid no heed to legal penalties, but rather the purity of my spirit and the cause of the city's disorders. I spoke about this, and we went about persuading the citizens. As a result three citizens were elected heads of the guilds, to aid the merchants and guildsmen whenever necessary.[4] These three were Bartolo di messer Iacopo de' Bardi, Salvi del Chiaro Girolami, and Rosso Bacherelli; they met in the church of San Procolo. The *popolani* became so emboldened when they saw that these three met with no opposition, and they were so aroused by the candid words of the citizens who spoke of their liberty and the injuries they had suffered, that they dared to make ordinances and laws which would have been hard to evade. They did not accomplish much else, but considering their weak beginning this was a great deal. These three officials were chosen for a term of two months starting June 15, 1282. When that term was finished, six officers were chosen, one for each sixth of the city, for a term of two months starting August 15, 1282. They were called the Priors of the Guilds; and they stayed secluded in the tower of the Castagna near the Badia so that they did not have to fear the threats of the powerful. They were given permission to carry arms *in perpetuo*, along with other privileges, and they were given six servants and six guards.

5 In essence, their laws stipulated that they should watch over the wealth of the Commune, that the magistrates should deal justly with everyone, and

---

4. On the development of the office of the Priors, see John M. Najemy, *Corporatism and Consensus in Florentine Electoral Politics 1280–1400* (Chapel Hill: University of North Carolina Press, 1982), 17ff.

that the small and weak should not be oppressed by the great and powerful. And keeping this arrangement would have been very good for the *popolo*. But things soon changed, since the citizens who held that office dedicated themselves not to keeping the laws, but rather to corrupting them. If one of their friends or relatives got into trouble, they arranged with the magistrates and officials to conceal their guilt, so that the lawbreakers might go unpunished. [Nor did they protect the wealth of the Commune, but rather sought better ways to plunder it] and so they drew great sums of money from the treasury of the Commune, under the pretext of rewarding men who had served it. Instead of being aided, the weak were attacked by the magnates and by the rich *popolani* who held office and were related by marriage to the magnates. And many were protected by bribery from the Communal penalties which they incurred. For these reasons the good *popolani* citizens were unhappy, and they blamed the office of the Priors, because the Guelf magnates had become lords.

6 At that time Arezzo was governed by the Guelfs and Ghibellines in equal portions; they shared evenly in the government, and they had sworn a firm peace among themselves.[5] Because of this the *popolo* rose up and named as Prior someone from the city of Lucca who led the *popolo* very successfully and compelled the nobles to obey the laws. The nobles then banded together and defeated the *popolo*; and they took the Prior and put him in a cistern, where he died.[6]

The Guelfs of Arezzo were urged by the Guelf Party of Florence to try to take control of the government, but either because they did not know how or because they were not able to do it, the Ghibellines realized what was afoot and chased them out of the city. They then came to Florence to complain about their enemies. Those who had given them this advice supported them and lent them aid. But no embassy or threat from Florence could persuade the Ghibellines to let them come home; and the Ghibellines of Arezzo sought the help of the Uberti, the Pazzi of the Valdarno, the Ubertini, and the Bishop of Arezzo, who was one of the Pazzi, a proud and spirited man who was better versed in the duties of war than those of the church.[7] Earlier,

5. Since 1282 the government of Arezzo had been shared equally by the Guelf and Ghibelline magnates; the *popolo* was excluded from any share in the government.

6. In 1287 the Guelfs and Ghibellines overthrew the government of the *popolo* and captured the Prior, messer Guelfo Falconi of Lucca. Accounts of his fate differ.

7. The bishop of Arezzo was Guglielmino degli Ubertini. The close relations between the Pazzi and the Ubertini may explain Compagni's error.

trouble had arisen between him and the Sienese over a castle which they had taken from him, and this issue had been referred to the Guelf Party of Florence. Because the Party wanted to help the Sienese and the exiles from Arezzo, and because they opposed the bishop, they provoked a great disagreement between the Florentines and the bishop and the Ghibellines. From this followed the third war of the Florentines in Tuscany, in 1289.

7   The powerful Florentine Guelfs were eager to go in arms to Arezzo, but many of the *popolani* disagreed, both because they thought the cause was unjust and because they were angry with the great Guelfs over the offices. Nonetheless they hired a captain named messer Baldovino di Soppino with four hundred horsemen; but the pope detained him and so he did not come.[8]

The Aretines summoned many noble and powerful Ghibellines from the Romagna, from the March of Ancona, and from Orvieto. They showed great eagerness for battle, and prepared to defend their city and to seize the advantage at the passes. The Florentines called on the people of Pistoia, Lucca, Bologna, Siena, and San Miniato and on the great captain Mainardo da Susinana, who was married to one of the della Tosa.

At this time King Charles of Sicily came to Florence on his way to Rome.[9] He was received honorably by the Commune with races and jousting, and he was asked by the Guelfs for one of his captains with the royal insignia. He left them his baron and gentleman messer Amerigo of Narbonne, who was young and fine looking but not well tested in arms. However, an old knight remained with him as his lieutenant, together with many other knights who were skilled and battle tested, and a great amount of money and provisions.

8   The bishop of Arezzo, wisely considering what might happen to him because of this war, sought to come to terms with the Florentines, leave Arezzo with his entire family, and pawn to the Florentines his castles within the bishopric. In exchange for his income and followers he wanted three thousand florins a year, which were promised to him by messer Vieri de' Cerchi, a very rich citizen. But there was sharp disagreement among the Priors who were in office at that time (messer Ruggieri da Cuona, a judge; messer Iacopo da Certaldo, judge; Bernardo di messer Manfredi Adimari;

8. The pope, Nicholas IV, was a supporter of the Ghibelline party.

9. King Charles II of Anjou passed through Florence early in May, 1289, on his way to the kingdom of Naples, which he had inherited on the death of his father, Charles I.

Pagno Bordoni; Dino Compagni, the author of this chronicle; and Dino di Giovanni, known as the Sheep), who held office from April 15 to June 15, 1289. The reason for their discord was that some of them wanted the bishop's castles and especially Bibbiena, so fine and strong, and others did not—nor did they want the war, considering what evil might come from it. Finally they all decided to accept the castles, but not to destroy them. They agreed to let Dino Compagni arrange matters as he thought best, because he was a good and intelligent man. He sent for messer Durazzo de' Vecchietti, who had recently been knighted by the bishop, and charged him to conclude negotiations with the bishop as best he could.

In the meantime the bishop of Arezzo thought that if he agreed to this arrangement, he would be a traitor. He therefore called together the leaders of his party and urged them to come to terms with the Florentines, and said that he did not want to lose Bibbiena, which should be strengthened and defended. Otherwise he himself would come to terms. Angered by his words, since all their plans were falling apart, the Aretines planned to have him killed; but his kinsman messer Guglielmo de' Pazzi—who was in the council—said that he would have been perfectly happy if they had done this without his knowledge, but, being asked, he would not agree to it, since he did not want to be a slayer of his own blood. Then they decided to take Bibbiena themselves, and like desperate men, they got themselves ready with no further deliberation.

9 When the Florentines heard of their decision, the war captains and governors held a meeting in the church of San Giovanni to discuss which route would be the best one to take, so that the camp might be supplied with whatever was needed. Some urged going by the Arno valley, since if they went by another route the Aretines would be able to ride there and burn the houses in the countryside. Others favored the route through the Casentino, saying that that was the better way and putting forward many reasons. A wise old man named Orlando da Chiusi and Sasso da Murli, great castellans who feared for their weak castles, advised that the latter route be chosen; they worried that if another route were taken, their castles (which were in the Aretine countryside) would be destroyed. And messer Rinaldo de' Bostoli, who was one of the exiles from Arezzo, agreed with them. There were plenty of speakers. They voted by secret ballot; the route through the Casentino won. And even though this route was the more doubtful and dangerous one, it turned out for the best.

After this deliberation, the Florentines gathered their allies. These were the Bolognese with two hundred horse; the Lucchese with two hundred; the Pistoiese with two hundred, led by the Florentine knight messer Corso Donati; Mainardo da Susinana with twenty horse and three hundred foot-soldiers; messer Malpiglio Ciccioni with twenty–five; and messer Barone Mangiadori of San Miniato, the Squarcialupi, and the people from Colle and other towns of the Val d'Elsa. In all there were 1,300 horse and plenty of infantry.

10   On the appointed day the Florentines unfurled their banners to go into enemy land. They passed through the Casentino by bad routes, where they would have suffered heavy losses if they had encountered enemies; but God willed otherwise. They arrived near Bibbiena, at a place called Campaldino, where their foes were, and there they stopped and formed their ranks. The war captains put the picked cavalry at the front of the formation, and the shields with the red lily on a white field were arrayed before them. Then the bishop, who was nearsighted, asked: "What are those walls?" He was told: "The shields of the enemy."

Messer Barone de' Mangiadori of San Miniato, a knight bold and expert in deeds of arms, gathered the soldiers and said to them: "Lords, the wars of Tuscany used to be won by a good charge and they didn't last long, and few men died in them because it was not the custom to kill them. But now tactics have changed and wars are won by standing firm. Because of this, I advise you to be strong and let them attack." And this they prepared to do. The Aretines attacked the camp so vigorously and with such force that the Florentine formation fell back considerably. The battle was very sharp and fierce; new knights were created on both sides. Messer Corso Donati with the Pistoiese squadron struck the enemy on the flank. The arrows rained down: the Aretines had few of them, and they were attacked on the flank, where they were unprotected.[10] The sky was covered with clouds; the dust was tremendous. The Aretine footsoldiers took knives in hand, threw themselves on all fours under the bellies of the horses, and disembowelled them. And some of their cavalry advanced so far that in the midst of our ranks many were killed on both sides. On that day many who had been considered brave proved to be cowards, and many who had been unknown won esteem. The captain's lieutenant showed great valor, and was killed. Messer Bindo del Baschiera della Tosa was wounded and so returned to Florence, but within a few days he died. On the enemy side the bishop, that bold knight messer

10. Count Guido Novello, who "did not wait for the end, but left without striking a blow," left the Aretine flank exposed.

Guglielmo de' Pazzi, Boncorte and Loccio da Montefeltro, and other worthy men were killed. Count Guido Novello did not wait for the end, but left without striking a blow. Messer Vieri de' Cerchi showed great prowess, as did his son the knight by his side. The Aretines were routed not out of cowardice or lack of prowess, but because of the overwhelming might of their foes. They were hunted down and killed: the Florentine mercenaries, who were accustomed to defeats, slaughtered them; the rural troops had no pity. Many Florentine *popolani* who owed cavalry service stayed put; many knew nothing until the enemies were routed. They did not rush to Arezzo after the victory since it was expected that they could take it with little effort.

The captain and the young knights, who needed rest, thought that they had done enough by winning without following up the victory. They captured banners from their enemies and took many prisoners; and they killed many of them, so that all Tuscany suffered harm.

This rout took place on June 11, the day of Saint Barnabas, at a place called Campaldino near Poppi.[11]

After this victory, however, not all of the Guelfs returned to Arezzo. Some of them ventured to return, and they were told that if they wanted to stay, they could do as they wished. The Florentines and Aretines did not make peace. The Florentines retained the castles they had taken—that is, Castiglione, Laterina, Civitella, Rondine, and many other castles—and razed some of them. After a little while the Florentines sent troops to Arezzo and pitched camp there. Two of the Priors went there: on Saint John's Day they held a horse race;[12] and they attacked the city and burned whatever they found in the countryside. Then they went to Bibbiena, and took it and razed the walls. The two Priors were greatly criticized for this excursion because this was not their job, but rather that of gentlemen accustomed to warfare. They subsequently returned with little gain, because the cost was great and the effort exhausting.

11 The citizens returned to Florence, and for several years the *popolo* was ruled in great and powerful state. But the nobles and the great citizens, swollen with pride, did many injuries to the *popolani*, beating them and committing other offenses. For this reason many good *popolani* and mer-

11. On the battle of Campaldino, in which the young Dante is supposed to have fought, see Herbert L. Oerter, "Campaldino, 1289," *Speculum*, 43 (1968), 429–450. Note that in his description of the battle Dino singles out Corso Donati and Vieri de' Cerchi, the two men who later in the chronicle will figure prominently as the leaders of the Black Guelfs and the Whites.

12. To celebrate the feast day of the patron saint of Florence.

chant citizens got together. Among them was one great and powerful citizen, that wise, worthy, and good man named Giano della Bella, a very spirited man from a good family, who disapproved of these offenses. Being one of the newly elected Priors who took office February 15, 1293, Giano made himself their leader; and with the help of the *popolo* and of his companions, he strengthened the *popolo*. They added to their office of Priors an office with the same authority as the others which they called the Standard-bearer of Justice (Baldo Ruffoli from the sixth of Porta Duomo). They gave him a banner with the arms of the *popolo*—that is, a red cross on a white field—and a thousand infantry all armed with that insignia or arms, who were to be ready at the Standard-bearer's every call, in the piazza or wherever he needed them. And they made laws which were called the Ordinances of Justice, directed against the powerful who might commit outrages against the *popolani*.[13] These Ordinances provided that each man be held responsible for his kinsmen, and that misdeeds could be proven by two attestations of public report and knowledge. And they decided that all members of any family that had included knights should be considered to be magnates, and that they could not be elected to be Priors or Standard-bearer of Justice, nor members of their councils. These families were in all seventy-three.[14] And they ordained that the outgoing Priors, together with certain additional officials, should elect the new ones. And they bound the twenty-four guilds to these arrangements by also giving some authority to their consuls.

12 The damned lawyers began to cavil about these laws which had been drawn up by messer Donato di messer Alberto Ristori, messer Ubertino dello Strozza, and messer Baldo Aguglioni. They said that where a crime was supposed to be punished "effectively" the laws exaggerated the crime to the harm of the accused; and that these laws frightened the magistrates, so that if the injured party were Ghibelline, the judge turned Ghibelline, and similarly with the Guelfs; and that members of the great families did not denounce their kin for fear of being punished. [But] few crimes were so hidden [by the magnates] that they were not discovered by their adversaries; many of them were punished in accordance with the law. The first who fell under the law were the Galligai, for one of them committed a crime

13. The first set of the Ordinances were approved on January 18, 1293, a month before Giano della Bella's term in office began.

14. There is a blank space left in the manuscript for the number of families declared to be magnates; perhaps Dino Compagni did not know the exact number. The number given here is taken from Gaetano Salvemini, *Magnati e popolani*, 376–377.

in France against two sons of a well-known merchant named Ugolino Benivieni. As a result of an argument one of these brothers was wounded by one of the Galligai, and he died of the wound. And I, Dino Compagni, being Standard-bearer of Justice in 1293, went to their houses and those of their kinsmen and had the former destroyed in accordance with the law.[15] This beginning led to a bad practice of the other Standard-bearers, because when according to the laws they were supposed to destroy something, the *popolo* called them cowards if they did not destroy it utterly. And many distorted justice for fear of the *popolo*. And so it happened that when a son of messer Buondelmonte committed a crime of murder, his houses were destroyed; but later he was compensated for them.

The arrogance of these wicked men grew great since the magnates, falling under these penalties, were punished and since the magistrates feared the laws which required them to punish "effectively." This "effectiveness" extended so far that they feared that if an accused man were not punished, the magistrates would have no defense or excuse; and so no one who was accused went unpunished. For these reasons the magnates complained vigorously about these laws and to the executors of the laws they said: "A horse runs and its tail hits the face of a *popolano*; or someone bumps into someone else in a crowd, meaning no malice; or a bunch of little children start to quarrel. Must they be destroyed for such a little thing?"

The aforesaid Giano della Bella, a strong and spirited man, was so bold that he upheld those things which others let drop, and spoke of those which others hushed up, and did everything in support of justice and against the guilty. He was so feared by the magistrates that they were afraid to conceal crimes. The magnates began to speak against him, accusing him of doing this not for justice but rather to kill his enemies, and attacking both him and the laws. Wherever they assembled, they threatened to butcher the *popolani* who were ruling. Some men who overheard this reported it to the *popolani*, who in turn began to grow bitter and out of fear and scorn they made the laws harsher, so that everyone was full of apprehension.[16] The leaders of the *popolo* were the Magalotti, since they had always been supporters of the

15. Other sources say that the first magnates to have their houses destroyed in accordance with the Ordinances of Justices were the Galli, not the Galligai, and that it was the first Standard-bearer of Justice, Baldo Ruffoli, who executed this sentence, not Dino Compagni, who was the third Standard-bearer. Compagni, writing twenty years after these events, may have confused the Galli and the Galligai; he may also have wished to exaggerate his own role in the events he described.

16. The Ordinances of Justice were reinforced for the first time on April 10, 1293, during the priorate of Giano della Bella.

popolo. They had a great following, and united around themselves many families which shared their outlook, and drew many petty tradesmen to their party.

13 The powerful citizens (who were not all noble by blood, but for other reasons were labeled magnates), out of scorn for the *popolo,* tried to attack it in many ways. They brought from Champagne a brave and bold knight named messer Jean de Châlons, a man more powerful than loyal, who had some jurisdictions given him by the emperor. He came to Tuscany allied with the magnates of Florence and by the will of the newly created Pope Boniface VIII. He held title and jurisdiction to whatever lands he might win. And men such as messer Vieri de' Cerchi and Nuto Marignolli agreed to this in order to crush the *popolo* of Florence, according to the report of messer Piero Cane of Milan, the procurator of the aforesaid messer Jean de Châlons. They laid many plans to kill Giano della Bella, saying: "When the shepherd is struck, the sheep will scatter."

One day they arranged to have him assassinated, but then they drew back for fear of the *popolo.* Next they craftily sought to bring about his death through more subtle maliciousness. They said: "He is a just man; bring to his attention the wicked deeds of the butchers, who are violent and disagreeable men." Among them was a person called the Sheep, a great butcher supported by the della Tosa, who practiced his trade in ways which were dishonest and harmful to the republic. He was prosecuted by his guild since he carried on his wicked practices brazenly. He threatened the magistrates and the officials, and dedicated himself to doing evil with a great force of men and arms.

Having gathered in the church of Ognissanti to revise the laws, those in the conspiracy against Giano della Bella said to him: "Look at what the butchers are doing and how their misdeeds are multiplying." And Giano replied: "May the city perish before this is tolerated," and he arranged to make laws against them. Similarly, they said of the jurists: "Look: the jurists threaten the magistrates with an audit and frighten them into granting unjust favors. And they keep cases pending for three or four years, and a decision is never rendered in any suit. They snarl up issues and penalties so much, without order, that someone who wants to abandon a case of his own will cannot do so." Giano, justly worrying about this, said: "Let there be laws to restrain such wickedness." And once they had set him ablaze about justice they secretly sent word to the jurists and butchers and other artisans, saying that Giano was vituperating them and making laws against them.

14 The conspiracy against Giano was uncovered one day when I, Dino, was meeting with several of them in Ognissanti and Giano was strolling in the garden. The conspirators drafted a deceptive law which not everyone understood: that any city or fortified place which received any banished enemy of the *popolo* should itself be considered an enemy. Since the conspiracy included traitorous *popolani*, they did this to put Giano under the bans and make him hated by the *popolo*. I recognized the plot and suspected why they formulated this law without the other companions. I revealed to Giano this conspiracy against him. I explained to him how they were making him an enemy of the *popolo* and of the artisans, and that if these laws were put into effect the *popolo* would turn against him, and that he should let the laws go and set to his defense with words. And so he did, saying: "May the city perish before so many wicked deeds are tolerated." Then Giano knew who was betraying him, for the conspirators could no longer conceal themselves. Those who were not guilty wanted to examine the facts prudently; but Giano, more brave than prudent, wanted to have them killed. And therefore we left off drafting the laws, and we parted in great discord.

The conspirators against Giano remained there: messer Palmieri di messer Ugo Altoviti and messer Baldo Aguglioni, jurists; Alberto di messer Iacopo del Giudice, Noffo di Guido Bonafedi, and Arriguccio di Lapo Arrighi. The notaries who took minutes were ser Matteo Biliotti and ser Pino da Signa. All the words said there were repeated in much worse form, so that the entire conspiracy hastened to kill him since they feared his works more than they feared him.

15 The magnates held their council in San Iacopo Oltrarno, and there everyone said that Giano must die. Then one representative from each household met, and messer Berto Frescobaldi was the speaker. He spoke of how these dogs of the *popolo* had stripped them of honors and offices, and how they did not dare to enter the public palace and could not press their suits. "If we beat one of our servants, we are undone. And therefore, lords, I recommend that we escape from this servitude. Let us take arms and run to the piazza. Let us kill as many of the *popolo* as we find, whether friends or enemies, so that never again shall we or our sons be subjugated to them."

Next messer Baldo della Tosa rose and said: "Lords, the advice of this wise knight is good—except that if our plan fell short we would all be killed. But let us first conquer them with cunning and sow discord among them with pious words, saying: 'The Ghibellines will take our city and chase out both them and us; for God's sake let them not allow the Ghibellines in the *signoria.'* And once they are divided, let us thrash them so that they will never rise again."

Everyone liked this knight's advice. They designated two men from each neighborhood to corrupt and sow discord among the *popolo*, and defame Giano, and detach from his side all the powerful among the *popolo* for the reasons given.

16 While the citizens concealed their true feelings, the city was in great discord. At this time it happened that messer Corso Donati, a powerful knight, sent some foot soldiers to wound his kinsman messer Simone Galastrone, and in the scuffle one of them was killed and others wounded. Both sides brought charges and it was therefore proper to proceed according to the Ordinances of Justice, by collecting testimony and punishing. The trial came before the podestà, messer Gian di Lucino, a Lombard and a noble knight of great wisdom and goodness. One of his judges, hearing the case and listening to the witnesses brought by both parties, understood that messer Corso was at fault. But he made the notary write the opposite so that messer Corso would be absolved and messer Simone condemned. As a result the podestà, being deceived, acquitted messer Corso and condemned messer Simone.

The citizens who heard what had happened thought that the podestà had been bribed to do this and that he was an enemy of the *popolo*. In particular, the adversaries of messer Corso cried with one voice: "Death to the podestà! To the flames, to the flames!" Taldo della Bella and Baldo dal Borgo were the ones who first started this furor, more out of dislike for messer Corso than out of concern for injured justice.[17] And the furor grew so great that the *popolo* dragged kindling to the palace of the podestà to burn its door.

Giano, who was with the Priors, hearing the cry of the crowd, said: "I want to go rescue the podestà from the hands of the *popolo*." He mounted his horse, believing that the *popolo* would follow him and draw back because of his words. But the opposite happened, for they turned their lances to knock him off the horse, so that he had to turn back. The Priors, to please the *popolo*, descended into the piazza with their banner, believing that this would calm the furor. But it grew so that they burned the door of the palace and stole the podestà's horses and belongings. The podestà fled to a nearby palace; his followers were captured. The records were torn up and every crafty person who had a case pending went to destroy them. Special care was

17. Taldo della Bella was the brother of Giano.

taken in this by one jurist named messer Baldo dell'Ammirato, who had many enemies and was in court with many complaints and lawsuits. Having cases against himself and fearing that he would be punished, he was so cunning that with his followers he broke open the cabinets and destroyed the documents so that they would never be found. Many people did strange things in that furor. The podestà and his followers were in great danger. He had brought with him his wife, who was well respected in Lombardy and very beautiful. Hearing the shouts of the *popolo*, she and her husband fled through the neighboring houses crying for their lives. There they found shelter and were concealed.

The council met the following day, and it was decided that for the honor of the city the stolen goods should be restored to the podestà and his salary should be paid. This was done, and he departed.

The city remained in great discord. The good citizens condemned what had been done. Some laid the blame on Giano, seeking to exile him or bring him to a bad end. Others said: "As long as we have begun, let's burn the rest." And there was such an uproar in the city that it fired everyone's minds against Giano. His relatives the Magalotti fell in with this. They advised him to leave the city for a few days to calm the furor of the *popolo*. He left, trusting their false advice; and without delay he was banished and his goods and person were condemned.

17 With Giano della Bella expelled on March 5, 1295 and his house pillaged and half destroyed, the *popolo minuto* lost all its pride and vigor for lack of a leader, and it could do nothing. The citizens named as podestà a person who had been Captain of the Popolo.[18] They began to bring charges against Giano's friends. Some of them were condemned—five hundred lire for this one, a thousand for that—and some refused to appear in court. Giano and his kindred left the country. The citizens remained in great discord, this one praising him and that one blaming him.

Messer Jean de Châlons, who had come at the request of the magnates, wanting to fulfill what he had promised and to acquire what he had been promised, asked for his pay for the five hundred horsemen he had brought with him. It was denied him, on the grounds that he had not accomplished what he had promised to do. This knight was a man of great spirit. He went off to Arezzo, to the adversaries of the Florentines, and said to them: "Lords,

18. Messer Guglielmo de' Maggi of Brescia, who from January 28 to March 6 replaced Gian di Lucino as podestà.

I came to Tuscany at the request of the Guelfs of Florence: here are the papers. They broke our agreement; because of this, my companions and I will help you fight them like mortal enemies." The Ubertini and the people of Arezzo and Cortona honored them for this.

The Florentines, hearing of this, sent to Pope Boniface, asking him to step in and arrange an accord between them. And he did so. He decided that the Florentines should give messer Jean twenty thousand florins, which they did. And since they were friends again, and seeing that the Aretines trusted him, the Florentines arranged with him that he should return to Arezzo and pretend to be our enemy. He was supposed to induce them to attack San Miniato, which he could claim belonged to him as representative of the Empire, and for which he had come and had a mandate. But someone who knew the secret revealed it out of flightiness and to show that he knew about secret things; and the person to whom he revealed it passed the information to messer Ceffo de' Lamberti. The Aretines heard of it through him and told the knight and his men to leave.

18 The *signori* who expelled Giano della Bella were Lippo del Velluto, the butcher Banchino di Giovanni, Gheri Paganetti, Bartolo Orlandini, messer Andrea da Cerreto, Lotto del Migliore Guadagni, and the Standard-bearer of Justice Gherardo Lupicini, who all entered office on February 15, 1295. The citizens began to accuse, condemn, and exile one another, so that Giano's friends were oppressed and cowed. Their adversaries lorded it over them with tremendous pride, accusing Giano and his followers of great presumption. They said that he had brought trouble to Pistoia when he was the magistrate there, and had burned villas and condemned many people. In fact, he should have received praise for these things because he had punished the exiles and evildoers who gathered there without fear of the laws. But they said that his just government had been tyranny. Many spoke ill of him out of cowardice and to gratify the wicked. The big butcher known as the Sheep—a liar, an inveterate evildoer, and a flatterer—dishonestly maligned him to please others. He corrupted the *popolo minuto*, formed conspiracies, and was so crafty that he persuaded the *signori* that they had been elected by his doing. He promised offices to many, and deceived them with these promises. He was a large man, bold and shameless, and a great chatterer. He openly named the conspirators against Giano, and said that he met with them in an underground vault. He was not very steadfast, and more cruel than just. He slandered Pacino Peruzzi, a man of good repute. He often harangued the councils without being invited and said that it was he who had freed them of the tyrant Giano and that many a night he had gone with a little lantern stirring people up to conspire against him.

19 For their protection, the worst citizens named as their podestà messer Monfiorito of Padua, a poor nobleman who would punish like a tyrant and make wrong out of right and right out of wrong, however they liked.[19] He quickly understood their wishes and obeyed them, so that he absolved and condemned without reason, at their whim. And he grew so bold that he and his followers sold justice openly and they scorned no offer, whether small or large. He became so hated that the citizens could not stand him, and they seized him and two of his followers and questioned them under torture. From his confession they learned things which brought plenty of shame and danger to many citizens. Then they began to disagree, because this one wanted to torture him some more and the other opposed it. One of them, named Piero Manzuolo, had him drawn up once more, as a result of which he confessed that he had accepted false testimony on behalf of messer Nicola Acciaiuoli and so had not condemned him. A note was made of this. When messer Nicola heard about this he was afraid that more might be revealed. He sought the advice of messer Baldo Aguglioni, his lawyer and a very clever jurist. Messer Baldo arranged to get the depositions from the notary to take a look at them, and he scratched out the part that went against messer Nicola.[20] The notary, suspecting that the depositions which he had loaned out had been tampered with, found the erasure and accused them. Messer Nicola was arrested and fined three thousand lire; messer Baldo fled, but was fined two thousand lire and put under bounds for a year. The rulers fell into great infamy. And there were many who in searching out criminals had found themselves; and they were unhappy about it for they were guilty.

Messer Monfiorito was thrown into prison.[21] The Paduans requested his release many times, but the Florentines would not release him for love or mercy. Finally he escaped from prison, because the wife of one of the Arrigucci, whose husband was in prison with him, provided some noiseless files and other tools with which they broke out of prison and fled.

19. Dino Compagni has skipped from 1295 to 1299. He errs slightly in identifying the podestà: all the other sources say that he was from Treviso.

20. This sort of sharp practice earned Baldo Aguglioni the condemnation of Dante. *Paradiso*, XVI, 56.

21. He had been removed from office by May 5, 1299, the date on which the Council of One Hundred decided to proceed against those who had corrupted the rulers, magistrates, and officials of the commune of Florence.

20 The city was ruled with little justice, and fell into fresh danger because the citizens became divided by competition for offices, each one hating his rival. It came about that some of the Cerchi family (men of low estate, but good merchants and very rich; they dressed well, kept many servants and horses, and made a brave show) bought the palace of the Counts [Guidi], near to the houses of the Pazzi and Donati, who were of more ancient lineage but not as rich.[22] The Donati, seeing the Cerchi rising—they had walled the palace and increased its height, and lived in high style—began to nurse a great hatred of them. Their hatred grew even greater when messer Corso Donati, a knight of great spirit whose wife had died, took for his new wife a daughter of the late messer Accierito da Gaville, who was her father's heir. Her relatives did not approve of this marriage because they hoped to receive this inheritance; but the girl's mother, seeing that messer Corso was a very handsome man, arranged the marriage against the will of the rest of the family.[23] The Cerchi, who were relatives of messer Neri da Gaville, began to get angry and tried to keep messer Corso from receiving her inheritance; but he took it by force. This gave rise to a great deal of turmoil and danger, both for the city and for private individuals. Once, when some young men of the Cerchi family were being held in the courtyard of the podestà as surety (as is the custom), they were given a black pudding of pork which made those who ate it seriously ill, and some of them died of it.[24] This provoked a great outcry in the city, for they were well liked and messer Corso was widely held to be responsible for this misdeed. There was no inquiry into this misdeed since nothing could be proven. But still the hatred grew day by day, so that the Cerchi began to avoid the Donati and the meetings of the [Guelf] Party and to align themselves with the *popolani* and the rulers. The Cerchi were well received by them, and likewise by the magistrates, both because they were men of great standing and humaneness and because they were very obliging, so that they could have whatever they wished from them. They drew with them many citizens, including the jurists messer Lapo Salterelli and messer Donato Ristori, and other powerful clans. The Ghibellines, too, loved the Cerchi for their humaneness and because they did them favors rather than harm. The *popolo minuto* loved them because they disapproved of the conspiracy against Giano della Bella. They were strongly

22. The Cerchi acquired this house in 1280.

23. Corso's new wife was Tessa, daughter of the late Ubertino degli Ubertini da Gaville; Compagni slips in recalling the name of the girl's father, but is correct in stating that she was his heir and that her relatives opposed the match, which was concluded in 1296.

24. This poisoning took place in 1298.

advised and urged to take the *signoria*, which because of their goodness they could easily have had; but they would never agree to it.

One day many citizens were gathered at the piazza of the Frescobaldi for the funeral of a woman.[25] At such gatherings, it was the custom of the city for ordinary citizens to be seated on the ground on rush mats, while knights and doctors [of law and medicine] were seated on benches. Those Donati and Cerchi who were not knighted were seated on the ground, the one party directly facing the other. One of them stood upright, either to straighten his clothes or for some other reason. His adversaries, out of suspicion, also stood up, and set hand to sword. The others did the same and they began to scuffle. The other men who were gathered there came between them and stopped the brawl. But things were not kept calm enough to prevent people from gathering at the houses of the Cerchi; and they would gladly have gone to hunt for the Donati, except that one of the Cerchi would not allow it.

There was a young nobleman named Guido, the son of the noble knight messer Cavalcante Cavalcanti; he was courtly and bold, but scornful, solitary, and studious.[26] He was an enemy of messer Corso and had often thought of harming him. Messer Corso feared him greatly, for he knew that he was very spirited; he tried to have Guido murdered while on a pilgrimage to Santiago de Compostella, but this was not carried out. Because of this, when Guido returned to Florence and learned of the plot, he stirred up against messer Corso many youths who promised to support him. And riding one day with some of the Cerchi household, with a dart in hand he spurred his horse against messer Corso, believing that the Cerchi would follow him and be drawn into the quarrel. As his horse ran past, he let fly the dart, which missed. There with messer Corso were his son Simone, a strong and brave youth, and Cecchino de' Bardi, and many others with their swords. They chased Guido but failed to catch him; they threw stones at him, and stones were thrown at him from the windows so that he was wounded in the hand.

As a result of this incident, the enmities began to spread. Messer Corso spoke very insultingly of messer Vieri de' Cerchi, calling him the ass of Porta San Piero, because he was a very good-looking man, but not very astute or articulate. And so he often used to say: "Has the ass of Porta San Piero brayed yet today?" He disparaged him greatly and called Guido a blockhead. All the jesters repeated this, especially one named Scampolino who exaggerated things when he repeated them, so that the Cerchi would

25. At the end of 1296.
26. He was also one of the best poets of Dante's generation.

be provoked to brawl with the Donati. The Cerchi did not take action, but threatened the Donati by becoming friendly with the Pisans and the Aretines. The Donati were frightened and said that the Cerchi had made league with the Ghibellines of Tuscany. And they defamed them so much that it came to the ears of the pope.

21 At that time the throne of St. Peter was occupied by Pope Boniface VIII, who was a man of great boldness and high intelligence; and he ruled the Church as he saw fit and brought low whoever did not agree with him. He was supported by his bankers, the Spini, a rich and powerful Florentine family. Simone Gherardi, a man well practiced in this business, resided in Rome as their agent; and with him was a Florentine named Nero Cambi, the son of a silver refiner, an astute man of subtle intelligence, but crude and unpleasant. This man worked so hard to convince the pope to lower the prestige of the Cerchi and their followers that the pope sent to Florence the friar messer Matteo di Acquasparta, cardinal of Porto, to pacify the Florentines. But the cardinal accomplished nothing because the factions would not grant him the powers he wanted, and so he left Florence in anger.

One St. John's Eve the guilds were going to make their customary offerings with their consuls at their head.[27] Some magnates laid hands on them and struck them, saying: "We are the ones who were responsible for the victory at Campaldino, yet you have taken from us the offices and honors of our city." The *signori*, angered, sought the advice of many citizens; and I, Dino, was one of them.[28] They confined some men of each faction. That is, of the Donati faction, messer Corso and Sinibaldo Donati, messer Rosso and messer Rossellino della Tosa, messer Giachinotto and messer Pazzino de' Pazzi, messer Geri Spini, messer Porco Manieri, and their relatives were confined to Castel della Pieve. And of the Cerchi faction, messer Gentile and messer Torrigiano and Carbone de' Cerchi, Guido Cavalcanti, Baschiera della Tosa, Baldinaccio Adimari, Naldo Gherardini, and some of their relatives were confined to Sarzana; and they obeyed and went where they were confined.

Those of the Donati faction did not want to leave, thus showing that there was a conspiracy among them. The magistrates wanted to condemn them.

27. On June 23, the vigil of the feast day of John the Baptist, the Florentine guilds used to march in procession to present offerings of wax, cloth, and so on to the saint.

28. The Priors at this time, June 15 to August 15, 1300, included Dante. When the officials had to make difficult decisions, like this one, they requested the opinions of leading citizens, both to benefit from their advice and to make them share responsibility for the decision.

And if they had not obeyed and had taken arms, that very day they would have conquered the city, since by arrangement with the Cardinal the Lucchese were coming to their aid with a great army of men.

When the *signori* saw that the Lucchese were coming, they wrote to warn them not to dare to enter our lands: and I was the one who drafted that letter. Our villagers were ordered to occupy the passes. And through the efforts of Bartolo di messer Iacopo de' Bardi, the Donati faction was persuaded to obey.

The wishes of the Cardinal were thus clearly revealed: the "peace" he sought was to bring low the Cerchi faction and raise up the Donati faction. His wishes were understood by many, and disliked thoroughly. And so someone who was not very bright picked up a crossbow and shot an arrow at the window of the bishop's palace (where the Cardinal was staying); it stuck in the shutter. The Cardinal left there out of fear, and for greater security he went to stay across the Arno at the house of messer Tommaso dei Mozzi.

As amends for the insult he had received the *signori* offered him two thousand florins. I brought them to him in a silver cup, and said: "My lord, do not disdain these because there are few of them, for we cannot give more money without [the vote of] the open council." He replied that he appreciated the offer; and he gazed at them for a long time, but did not take them.

22 Because the young are easier to deceive than the old, the devil—that sower of evils—made use of a band of youths who used to ride around together. These youths gathered for dinner one evening, on the first of May, and they grew so arrogant that they decided to confront the Cerchi band and use their fists and swords against them.[29] On that evening, which marks the return of spring, the ladies were accustomed to hold dances in the neighborhoods. The Cerchi youths encountered the Donati band, which included a nephew of messer Corso, Bardellino de' Bardi, Piero Spini, and other companions and followers, who attacked the Cerchi band with arms in hand. In that assault Ricoverino de' Cerchi's nose was slashed by one of the Donati followers (it was said to be Piero Spini, in whose home they took refuge). This blow caused the destruction of our city, because it increased the great hatred between the citizens. The Cerchi never revealed who struck the blow, but waited to make a great vendetta.

The city was divided anew: the great, middling, and little men and even

29. Having carried his narrative to July 1300 in the preceding chapter, Compagni here turns back to the incident two months earlier which marked the open break between the Cerchi and the Donati.

the clergy could not help but give themselves wholeheartedly to these factions, this man to one and that to the other. All the Ghibellines sided with the Cerchi because they hoped to receive less harm from them, and so did all those who had been of Giano della Bella's mind, since the Cerchi had appeared to mourn his exile. Also of their party were Guido di messer Cavalcante Cavalcanti, because he was an enemy of messer Corso Donati; Naldo Gherardini, because he was an enemy of the Manieri, relatives of messer Corso; messer Manetto Scali and his family, because they were relatives of the Cerchi; messer Lapo Salterelli, their kinsman; messer Berto Frescobaldi, because he had received large loans from them; messer Goccia Adimari, because he was their business associate; messer Biligiardo, Baschiera, and Baldo della Tosa, out of dislike for their kinsman messer Rosso, because thanks to him they had been deprived of their honors. The Mozzi, the main branch of the Cavalcanti, and many other great families and *popolani* sided with them.

With the party of messer Corso Donati sided messer Rosso, messer Arrigo, messer Nepo, and Pinuccio della Tosa, out of long familiarity and friendship; messer Gherardo Ventraia, messer Geri Spini and his relatives, because they had offended the Cerchi; messer Gherardo Sgrana and messer Bindello, out of familiarity and friendship; messer Pazzino de' Pazzi and his relatives, the Rossi, most of the Bardi, the Bordoni, the Cerretani, Borgo Rinaldi, Manzuolo, the Sheep the butcher, and many others.

Among the *popolani* who sided with the Cerchi were the Falconieri, the Ruffoli, the Orlandini, the delle Botte, the Angiolieri, the Amuniti, the family of Salvi del Chiaro Girolami, and many other *popolani grassi*.

23 Messer Corso Donati was confined to Massa Trabaria, but he did not obey; he broke his bounds and went off to Rome, for which he was condemned in his goods and his person. Together with Nero Cambi, who was the Spini representative at the Papal Court, and through the mediation of messer Iacopo Caetani (a kinsman of the pope) and some of the Colonna, he insistently begged the pope to remedy the situation because the Guelf Party in Florence was being destroyed while the Cerchi supported the Ghibellines. As a result, the pope summoned messer Vieri de' Cerchi who went very honorably to Rome. At the request of his bankers the Spini and of the aforementioned friends and relatives, the pope asked him to make peace with messer Corso. However, messer Vieri would not agree to this, but explained that he was doing nothing against the Guelf Party. He was then given leave to go and he departed.

The Cerchi faction, which had been exiled to Sarzana, returned to Florence. Messer Torrigiano, Carbone, and Vieri di messer Ricovero de' Cerchi, messer Biligiardo della Tosa, Carbone and Naldo Gherardini, messer Guido Scimia de' Cavalcanti, and the others of that party remained tranquil.[30]

But the leaders of the other faction—messer Geri Spini, messer Porco Manieri, messer Rosso della Tosa, messer Pazzino de' Pazzi, Sinibaldo di messer Simone Donati—were displeased by the Cerchi's homecoming, and they met one day with their followers in Santa Trinità, where they plotted to expel the Cerchi and their party. They held a large meeting, advancing many false justifications; and after a long discussion messer Buondelmonte, a wise and temperate knight, said that it was too great a risk and that too much evil could come from it and that for the present it should not be permitted. And the majority went along with this opinion although messer Lapo Salterelli had promised Bartolo di messer Iacopo de' Bardi (in whom great faith was placed) that things would be arranged in good fashion. And they left without doing anything.

24 I, Dino Compagni, attended that meeting. Since I wanted unity and peace among the citizens, I said before they left: "Lords, why do you want to disturb and ruin so good a city? Against whom do you wish to fight— against your brothers? What victory would you have? Nothing but mourning." They replied that their meeting was meant only to settle conflicts and preserve peace.

Having heard this, I approached Lapo di Guaza Ulivieri, a good and loyal *popolano*, and together we went to the Priors. We brought with us some men who had been at that meeting and we acted as intermediaries between them and the Priors and mollified the *signori* with soft words. Messer Palmieri Altoviti, who was then one of the *signori*, reproached these men strongly but without threats. They assured the *signori* that nothing more would come of that meeting, and asked that certain footsoldiers who had come at their request be allowed to depart without being harmed. And this was commanded by the lord Priors.

The opposing party constantly urged the *signoria* to punish the Donati, for in this meeting in Santa Trinità they had contravened the Ordinances of Justice by making a conspiracy and a plot against the government.

In investigating the truth of this conspiracy, it was discovered that the Count of Battifolle had sent his son with his armed followers at the request

30. This Guido Scimia de' Cavalcanti is not the Guido Cavalcanti who was so hated and feared by Corso Donati; that Guido Cavalcanti died in August 1300, while in exile.

of the conspirators. And letters were found in which messer Simone de' Bardi had written that he would have a great quantity of bread baked, so that the men who were coming would have enough to eat. This clearly proved that a conspiracy was arranged at that meeting in Santa Trinità, for which the Count and his son and messer Simone were sentenced to heavy penalties.

Now that the hatred and ill will of both factions were out in the open, each group strove to harm the other. But in their harsh words the Donati revealed themselves much more brazenly than the Cerchi, and they feared nothing.

25   The Cerchi worked to get the Pistoiese on their side. The Pistoiese had given the Florentines jurisdiction over their city and asked them to provide the podestà and captain. The Florentines sent as captain Cantino di messer Amadore Cavalcanti, an unreliable man who broke the Pistoiese law which stipulated that their Elders should be chosen from both of their parties, that is, from the Blacks and the Whites. These two parties, Blacks and Whites, originated from a family called the Cancellieri which had split: some who were closely related were called the Whites, and the rest the Blacks; and eventually the whole city was divided. And they elected the Elders according to this division.

This Cantino broke their law and had all the Elders selected from the White faction. When he was criticized for this, he said in his defense that he had been ordered to do this by the *signori* of Florence. But he was not telling the truth.

The unhappy Pistoiese lived in great turmoil, injuring and killing each other. They were often fined and treated harshly by their magistrates, both justly and unjustly, and a lot of money was squeezed from them. However, the Pistoiese are by nature disagreeable, cruel, and savage men. Messer Ugo Tornaquinci, the podestà, took from them three thousand florins through fines of this sort, and many other Florentine citizens who were magistrates there acted similarly.

Giano della Bella had been captain there. He ruled them honestly but harshly, for he burned the houses outside the city where they received exiles in violation of the decrees.

There was in Pistoia a dangerous knight of the party of the Black Cancellieri named messer Simone da Pantano, a man of medium height, thin and dark, pitiless and cruel, a robber who was willing to do any wicked deed. He was of the party of messer Corso Donati. Allied with the opposing party was someone named messer Schiatta Amati, a man more cautious than wise, and less cruel; he was related to the White Cerchi.

At this time the Florentines knighted Andrea Gherardini and sent him to Pistoia as captain. Messer Andrea was convinced that the Lucchese were coming to attack Pistoia, and this prompted him to exile many citizens. They did not leave willingly at his command, but instead gathered their forces and sought to defend themselves, believing that they would find support. Messer Simone da Pantano assembled many friends and foreign troops. The podestà set a deadline for their departure which they did not obey; so he grew angry and punished them with fire and sword, with Florentine assistance, and he declared their followers rebels. Some said that the Whites gave messer Andrea four thousand florins to do this, and others said that the money came from the Commune of Florence, to compensate him for the enemies he had made by his actions.

26 What a good and beautiful and prosperous city has been ruined![31] Let its citizens lament—citizens who are more handsome than other Tuscans and owners of such a rich place, surrounded by lovely streams and fertile hills and fine lands. They are strong in arms, but discordant and savage, and that was what brought a city like this to the brink of death. For in just a short time their fortunes changed and they were besieged by the Florentines—besieged so closely that they gave their flesh to get food and allowed themselves to be maimed in order to bring supplies to their city, and they were brought to such a state that they had consumed even their last day's supply of bread. God in His glory provided for them, when (without the knowledge of their adversaries) they agreed to surrender on terms which guaranteed their safety. These terms were not honored, for as soon as the city was taken, its beautiful walls were cast down.

Though the victors had stopped the pestilential cruelty of cutting off the noses of the women who left the city out of hunger (they cut off the hands of the men), they did not spare the beauty of the city, which they left like a ruined village. But I do not intend to write of this siege, nor of Pistoia's peril and hunger, nor of the assaults and the brave deeds of those who closed themselves in there, nor of the fine castles which they lost through treason, for someone else will write of this more accurately. And if he writes of it with compassion, he will make his listeners weep uncontrollably.

31. The expulsion of the Blacks from Pistoia moved Dino Compagni to consider its result: the bitter siege of Pistoia conducted by the Florentine Blacks in 1306, which he describes at greater length in III, 13–15.

27   When messer Andrea's term in office was over, the White faction of Florence did not know how to govern itself because it lacked a leader, since the Cerchi shunned the desire for even the title of lordship (more out of cowardice than humility, for they greatly feared their adversaries). They invited messer Schiatta Amati of the White Cancellieri to be their war captain and gave him authority to command the soldiers, issue decrees in his own name, and impose penalties and arrange expeditions against enemies without holding a council. This knight was very pliable and timid, and he did not care for war. In every way he was the opposite of his kinsman, messer Simone da Pantano of the Black Cancellieri.

This captain did not grip the city as he should have, and his enemies did not fear him. The soldiers went unpaid; they had neither money nor the courage to raise any. He took no fortresses and exiled no one. He spoke threatening words and made a great show, but to no effect. Those who lacked insight thought that the Cerchi were rich and powerful and wise, and for this reason were full of confidence. But the wise men said: "They are merchants and so they are cowards by nature, whereas their enemies are masters of war and ruthless men."

The enemies of the Cerchi began to complain about them to the Guelfs, saying that the Cerchi had reached an understanding with the Aretines and Pisans and with the Ghibellines. This was not true, for they had no pact with the Ghibellines, nor even any friendship. Yet many people turned against them and levelled this false charge; and whenever the Cerchi were accused they did not deny it, since they believed that this would make them more feared and would strike at their foes. The Cerchi thought: "They will fear us more, out of worry that we will ally with the Ghibellines; and the Ghibellines will love us more, out of hope in us." And so the Cerchi, who wanted to rule, ended by being ruled, as I shall explain.

BOOK II

1   Arise, wicked citizens full of discord: grab sword and torch with your own hands and spread your wicked deeds. Unveil your iniquitous desires and your worst intentions. Why delay any longer? Go and reduce to ruins the beauties of your city. Spill the blood of your brothers, strip yourselves of faith and love, deny one another aid and support. Sow your lies, which will fill the granaries of your children. Do as did Sulla in the city of Rome. Yet all the evils that Sulla achieved in ten years, Marius avenged in a few days: do you believe that God's justice has faltered since then? Even the justice of this world demands an eye for an eye. Look at your ancestors: did they win merit through discord? Yet now you sell the honors which they acquired. Do not delay, wretches: more is consumed in one day of war than is gained in many years of peace, and a small spark can destroy a great realm.

2   The citizens of Florence, divided like this, began to slander one another throughout the neighboring cities and in Pope Boniface's court at Rome, spreading false information.[1] And words falsely spoken did more damage to Florence than the points of swords. They worked on the pope, telling him that the city would return to the hands of the Ghibellines and become a bastion for the Colonna,[2] and they reinforced these lies with a great deal of money. The pope was persuaded to break the power of the Florentines, and so he promised to aid the Black Guelfs with the great power of Charles of

---

1. That is, the Black Guelfs defamed the Whites and complained about them to the pope.
2. The Colonna, one of the most powerful families in Rome, were (with the exception of the branch mentioned in I, 23) bitter enemies of Boniface VIII.

Valois, of the royal house of France, who had set out from France to oppose Frederick of Aragon in Sicily.[3] The pope wrote that he wanted messer Charles to make peace in Tuscany, opposing those who had rebelled against the Church. This commission of peacemaker had a very good name, but its purpose was just the opposite, for the pope's aim was to bring down the Whites and raise up the Blacks, and make the Whites enemies of the royal house of France and of the Church.

3 Since messer Charles had already arrived at Bologna, the Blacks of Florence sent ambassadors to deliver this message: "My lord, have mercy for God's sake. We are the Guelfs of Florence, faithful servants of the king of France. For God's sake, look out for yourself and your men, for our city is ruled by Ghibellines."

After the ambassadors of the Blacks had left, the Whites arrived with the greatest reverence and gave messer Charles many gifts, as if he were their lord. But the malicious words carried more weight with messer Charles than the true ones, for to him saying "watch where you're going" seemed a greater sign of friendship than did gifts. He was advised to come by way of Pistoia, so that he might fall out with the Pistoiese. The Pistoiese wondered why he should take that route, and out of fear they guarded the city gates with hidden weapons and men. Then the sowers of discord said to messer Charles: "My lord, do not enter Pistoia, for they will take you prisoner. They have armed the city secretly, and they are very bold men and enemies of the house of France." And they filled him with such fear that he bypassed Pistoia and followed a little rivulet, thus displaying his hostility to the city. And this fulfilled the prophecy of an ancient peasant, who long ago had said: "From the west along the Ombroncello will come a lord who will do great things. Because of his coming, beasts of burden will walk on the peaks of Pistoia's towers."[4]

4 Without entering Florence, messer Charles traveled on to the papal court in Rome. There he was greatly aroused and many suspicions were planted in his mind. This lord did not understand the Tuscans or their malice. Messer Muciatto Franzesi, a very wicked knight, small in stature but great in spirit, knew full well the malice behind the words said to his lord;

3. Charles of Valois, brother of King Philip IV of France, left for Italy in the summer of 1301; his intention was to assist the Angevins and the Church in the reconquest of Sicily, which in 1282 had rebelled against the Angevins and accepted Aragonese rule.

4. This prophecy was fulfilled five years later, in 1306, when the Florentine Blacks took Pistoia and demolished its walls. See below, III, 15.

but because he too was corrupt he confirmed everything that was said by the sowers of discord who surrounded messer Charles every day.

The White Guelfs had ambassadors at the Papal Court of Rome together with the Sienese, but they were not sound men. Some of them were actually harmful: one such person was messer Ubaldino Malavolti, a Sienese[5] jurist and a man full of cavilings, who stopped on the journey to demand the return of certain jurisdictions belonging to a castle which the Florentines held, saying that they pertained to him. And he so delayed the journey of his companions that they did not arrive in time.[6]

When the ambassadors did arrive in Rome, the pope received them privately in his chambers and said to them in secret: "Why are you so obstinate? Humble yourselves to me. I can truthfully say that I have no intention other than to make peace among you. Let two of you return home, and they shall have my blessing if they see to it that my will is obeyed."

5   At that time new *signori* were elected in Florence, more or less unanimously by both parties. They were good men who were not suspect and the *popolo minuto* placed great hope in them. So too did the White Party, because the new *signori* were free of arrogance and supporters of unity and they wished to apportion the offices fairly, saying: "This is the final remedy."

Their enemies also took hope from them, for they knew the new *signori* to be weak and peace-loving men, and believed they could easily delude them with the semblance of peace.

These *signori* who took office on October 15, 1301 were: Lapo del Pace Angiolieri; Lippo di Falco Cambio; myself, Dino Compagni; Girolamo di Salvi del Chiaro; Guccio Marignolli; Vermiglio di Iacopo Alfani; and Piero Brandini, Standard-bearer of Justice. When their names were drawn, they went to Santa Croce, for their predecessors' turn in office was not finished.[7] The Black Guelfs immediately arranged to go visit them in groups of four or six at a time. They said: "Lords, you are good men and our city needs such men. You can see the discord of your fellow citizens: it is up to you to pacify them, or the city will perish. You are the ones who have the authority; and to help you exercise it we offer you our goods and persons, in good and loyal spirit." I, Dino, replied by commission of my companions, and said: "Dear and faithful citizens, we willingly accept your offers and would like to begin

5. An error: he was actually from Bologna.
6. That is, by the time they arrived, the words of the Blacks had already done their damage.
7. The names of the new *signori* were drawn on the seventh of the month, eight days before the old term in office ended.

to put them to use. We ask you to counsel us and set your minds to it, so that our city can be calmed." And so we wasted time, since we did not dare to shut the doors and stop listening to these citizens—even though we distrusted such false promises and thought that they were cloaking their malice with lying words.

We sought to make peace with them when we should have been sharpening our swords. And we began with the Captains of the Guelf Party, messer Manetto Scali and messer Neri Giandonati, saying to them: "Honorable Captains, put everything else aside. Leave it, and work only to bring peace to the Party of the Church, and we will put our office entirely at your disposal in any way you desire."

The Captains left very happy and in good spirits, and they began to persuade men and speak compassionate words. The Blacks, hearing this, at once called this malice and treason and they began to flee from these words.

Messer Manetto Scali was so courageous that he tried to arrange peace between the Cerchi and the Spini; and all this was held to be treason. The people who sided with the Cerchi became timid because of this: "We do not need to trouble ourselves since peace is coming." And all the while their enemies planned to bring their malice to fruition. No preparation was made for battle, since for many reasons the Whites could think of nothing but achieving concord. The first reason was love of the Guelf Party and unwillingness to share the offices of the city with Ghibellines. The second reason was that even though there was nothing but discord, the injuries were not yet so widespread that concord could not be restored if they shared the offices evenly [between the Guelf factions]. But the Blacks thought that those who had made enemies could not escape vengeance unless the Cerchi and their followers were destroyed; and the Cerchi power was so great that they could hardly do this without destroying the city.

6   The Black Guelfs planned and arranged to have messer Charles of Valois, who was at the Papal Court, come to Florence; they deposited seventy thousand florins to hire him and his knights, and brought him as far as Siena.[8] Once he had arrived there, he sent as ambassadors to Florence his chancellor, the Frenchman messer Guglielmo—an untrustworthy and wicked man, although in appearance he seemed good and benign—and a Provençal knight who was just the opposite, with letters from their lord.

When they arrived in Florence, they visited the Signoria with great reverence and sought and obtained permission to address the Great Council. In

8. Charles arrived at Siena on October 14, 1301.

the council a lawyer from Volterra who accompanied them spoke on their behalf. This man was dishonest and rather stupid, and he spoke very confusedly. He said that the royal blood of France had come to Tuscany for the sole purpose of bringing peace to the Party of Holy Church, out of great love for the city and that party. The pope had sent messer Charles because he was a lord in whom one could trust, for the blood of the house of France never betrayed friend or enemy. The Florentines should therefore be pleased that he had come as peacemaker.

Many speakers rose to their feet, eager to speak in praise of messer Charles, and each of them rushed to the rostrum to be the first to respond. The *signori* let no one speak, but there were so many that the ambassadors realized that the faction which welcomed messer Charles was larger and bolder than the faction which opposed him. And so they wrote to their lord that they could see that the Donati faction had risen a great deal, while the Cerchi had fallen.

The *signori* told the ambassadors that they would send an embassy to answer messer Charles. In the meantime they took counsel: this was such a new development that they did not want to do anything without the agreement of their citizens.

7 Accordingly, they called a general council of the Guelf Party and of the seventy-two craft guilds, all of which had consuls, and they asked each one to submit a written statement on whether his guild wanted messer Charles of Valois to come to Florence as peacemaker.[9] They all replied, in speech and in writing, that he should be allowed to come and should be honored like a lord of noble blood—all except the bakers, who said that he should be neither received nor honored, for he was coming to destroy the city.

They sent to messer Charles ambassadors who were great citizens of the *popolo*, to say that he was free to enter. They were charged to obtain from him sealed letters promising that he would not exercise any jurisdiction over us, nor occupy any city office, whether by imperial title or any other means, nor tamper with the laws or customs of the city. The speaker was messer Donato di Alberto Ristori; he was accompanied by many other jurists. Messer Charles's chancellor was asked to request his lord not to come on All

9. Only twenty-one guilds were constituted with full rights of participating in the government of Florence. The much larger number given here must include other trade groups which, despite having their own consuls, were normally affiliated with or subordinated to the twenty-one guilds. The inclusion of a far wider segment of the populace than was usually allowed to participate in political life indicates the importance assigned to the choice which now faced Florence.

Saints' Day, because on that day the *popolo minuto* holds a festival with the new wine and many disturbances could break out which, with the malice of the wicked citizens, might throw the city into turmoil. Because of this messer Charles decided to come the following Sunday, judging that this delay was for the best.

The ambassadors went more to obtain this letter before his arrival than for any other reason. They were warned that if he did not deliver it as he had promised they should take it as a sign of his bad faith and therefore block his passage at Poggibonsi, which had been reinforced to protect the city. And messer Bernardo de' Rossi, who was vicar there, was empowered to deny him provisions. At this time the letter arrived, and I saw it and had it copied, and I held it until the arrival of the lord. And when he had arrived I asked him if it had been written at his will; he replied: "Yes, of course."

Those who had hired messer Charles made haste and drew him from Siena almost by force; they gave him seventeen thousand florins to hurry him along, for he feared the wrath of the Tuscans and proceeded very cautiously. They encouraged him and his people, saying: "Lord, they are beaten, and they seek to delay your coming for some malice, and they are hatching plots." And they planted other suspicions in his mind. But no plot was being made.

8   With things in this state, a good and holy thought came to me, Dino. I reflected: "This lord will come and he will find all the citizens divided, which will cause great disturbances." Because of the office which I held and the good will which I sensed in my companions, I thought of assembling many good citizens in the baptistery of San Giovanni; and I did so. All the magistrates were there, and when I thought it was time, I said: "Dear and worthy citizens, who have all alike received sacred baptism at this font, reason compels and binds you to love one another like dear brothers, especially since you possess the most noble city in the world. Some enmity has sprung up among you over competition for offices—offices which, as you know, my companions and I have promised on our oaths to apportion equally. Now this lord Charles is coming and he should be received honorably. Set aside these enmities and make peace among yourselves so that he does not find you divided. Set aside all the grudges and wicked desires that you have harbored till now. Let everything be forgiven and set aside, for love and the good of your city. And on this sacred font, where you received holy baptism, swear a good and perfect peace among yourselves, so that the lord who is coming may find all the citizens united."

Everyone agreed with these words and acted upon them. While physically touching the book, they swore to uphold peace in good faith and to preserve the offices and governance of the city. When this was done, we left that place.

Those wicked citizens, who there displayed tears of tenderness and kissed the book and showed the most ardent good will, proved to be the leaders in the destruction of their city. Out of goodness I will not mention their names, but I cannot conceal the name of the first oathtaker because he was the one who moved the rest to follow. This was Rosso dello Strozza, wild in appearance and actions, the instigator of the rest; he soon felt the weight of his oath.

Men of ill will said that this charitable peace had been founded on deceit. If there was any fraud in the words, I must suffer the penalty for it, although good intentions should not be rewarded with injury. I have shed many tears over this oath, thinking how because of it so many souls were damned for their malice.[10]

9   Messer Charles arrived in the city of Florence on Sunday, November 4, 1301 and the citizens honored him greatly with races and jousting.[11] The party of unity lost its vigor; the malice began to spread. The Lucchese came to the city, saying that they came to honor the lord; the Perugians came with two hundred horse; messer Cante da Gubbio came with many Sienese knights; and many others came, six or ten at a time, all of them foes of the Cerchi.[12] Entrance was not denied even to Malatestino or to Mainardo da Susinana, so as not to displease the lord. And each of them pretended to be our friend. With his own eight hundred horse and those that came from the surrounding country, messer Charles had twelve hundred horse at his command.

The lord lodged in the Frescobaldi house.[13] He had been urged to lodge at

10. By persuading them to swear this solemn oath which they later broke, Dino Compagni had unintentionally helped transform their feigned reconciliation into the sin of perjury.

11. The date given here is incorrect. November 4 was a Saturday, not a Sunday. And all of the other sources say that Charles entered Florence on November 1 as originally planned; the Blacks evidently persuaded him not to observe the delay (if, indeed, Compagni is correct in saying that he had agreed to delay his entrance). For the problems entailed by this error, see below, II, 15.

12. Messer Cante de' Gabrielli da Gubbio had already been podestà in Florence in 1298. He was podestà again a few months later, when he sentenced Dante and other leaders of the White Guelfs to exile. See below, II, 25.

13. The Frescobaldi house was located across the Arno, near the Santa Trinità bridge.

Santa Maria Novella, where the great and honored King Charles and all the great lords who came to the city stayed, since there was ample room and the place was safe.[14] But the men who led him did otherwise: they arranged instead to fortify themselves with him across the Arno, thinking: "If we lose the rest of the city, we can regroup our forces here."

10 The lord Priors chose forty citizens from both factions and consulted with them about the safety of the city, so that they would not be held suspect by either faction. Those with bad intentions kept silent; the others had lost their strength.

Bandino Falconieri, a vile man, said: "Lords, I feel fine, whereas before I did not sleep securely," thus displaying his cowardice to his adversaries. He kept the rostrum blocked up half the day, and we were in the shortest days of the year.

Messer Lapo Salterelli feared the pope very much because of the harsh charges the pope had lodged against him, and he wanted to improve his relations with his foes. So he took the rostrum and accused the Priors, saying: "You are destroying Florence. Choose new *signori* from both factions and let the exiles come home to the city." And in his house he had messer Pazzino de' Pazzi, who was exiled, trusting that messer Pazzino would protect him when he returned to power.

Alberto del Giudice, a rich *popolano*, melancholy and spoiled, mounted the rostrum and blamed the *signori* because they did not hasten to choose new *signori* and bring the exiles home. Messer Lotteringo da Montespertoli said: "Lords, do you want some advice? Choose new *signori* and return the exiles to the city, and then take the gates off their hinges. That is, if you do these two things, you can have the locks removed from the gates."

I asked messer Andrea da Cerreto, a wise jurist from an old Ghibelline family who had become a Black Guelf, if one could name new *signori* without violating the Ordinances of Justice. He replied that it could not be done. And I, who had been accused and charged with violating those ordinances, undertook to uphold them and not let new *signori* be named illegally.[15]

14. Charles I of Anjou, king of Sicily, stayed at the Dominican convent of Santa Maria Novella on his first visit to Florence, in 1267; so too did Cardinal Latino in 1280. At this time Santa Maria Novella lay outside the city walls, which were in the process of being extended.

15. Compagni alludes here to a charge made against him in 1295, in the aftermath of Giano della Bella's exile, of having failed to apply the sanctions of the Ordinances of Justice against certain magnates during his tenure as Standard-bearer of Justice in 1293. Nothing came of this accusation.

11 At this time the two ambassadors returned from seeing the pope. One was Maso di messer Ruggierino Minerbetti, a false *popolano* who did not stand by his own opinion but followed that of others; the other was Corazza da Signa, who considered himself so Guelf that he hardly believed that the Guelf spirit was still alive in anyone else. They reported the pope's words. I was then responsible for holding back this message. I held it back and swore the ambassadors to secrecy; but it was not out of malice that I delayed it. I assembled six wise jurists and had the message repeated before them, and did not allow open discussion. At the will of my companions, I proposed and advised and decided that we should obey this lord [the pope], and that we should immediately write to him that we were at his disposal and that he should send us the cardinal messer Gentile da Montefiore to establish order.

The pope sent enticing words with one hand and with the other set this lord over us; once he saw that messer Charles had entered the city, he stopped his blandishments and used threats. One of the ambassadors betrayed us and revealed the papal message, which the others should not have been able to hear. And Simone Gherardi had written to them from the Papal Court, saying that the pope had told him: "I do not want to lose men for weak women."

The Black Guelfs took counsel over this. They judged from these words that the ambassadors had come to an agreement with the pope, and said: "If they are united, we are lost." They thought they should wait and see what action the Priors would take, saying: "If they reject the pope's offer, we are dead; if they accept it, let us seize our swords and take from them whatever we can." And so they did. As soon as they heard that the magistrates would obey the pope they immediately armed themselves and began to attack the city with fire and sword, devastating and destroying it.

The Priors wrote to the pope in secret, but the Black Party knew everything since those who swore secrecy did not keep it. The Black Party had two leaders, who were not known to outsiders; their term in office lasted six months. One of them was Noffo Guidi, a wicked and cruel *popolano* who did the worst for his city. His usual practice was to denounce in public the things he did in secret, and to blame others for them. Because of this he was thought to be good and temperate, and so he profited from his evildoing.

12 The leading citizens pressed the *signori* to name new *signori*. Although this was against the Ordinances of Justice, since it was not yet time to select new *signori*, we agreed to name them, more for love of the city than for any other reason. I went to the chapel of San Bernardo on behalf of all the *signori* and assembled there many *popolani*, including the most powerful ones, without whom nothing could be done.[16] These were Cione Magalotti, Segna Angiolini, and Noffo Guidi for the Black Party and messer Lapo Falconieri, Cece Canigiani, and Corazza Ubaldini for the White Party. I spoke to them humbly and with great compassion about saving the city, saying: "I want to make the offices common to all, since competition for offices creates so much discord." We all agreed and elected six citizens in common, three from the Blacks and three from the Whites. As for the seventh, since it could not be split, we chose someone of so little value that no one feared him. I placed the written names on the altar. Then Noffo Guidi spoke, and said: "I am going to say something, though you will consider me a cruel citizen." I told him to be quiet. But he spoke nonetheless and was so arrogant as to ask me to please give their party a greater share of the *signori* than the other—which was as much as to say "destroy the other party" and put me in the position of Judas. I replied that I would feed my children to the dogs before I committed such treason. And so we ended the meeting.

13   Messer Charles of Valois often invited us to dine with him. We replied that according to our oath of office the law constrained us from accepting his invitation (which was true), since among ourselves we suspected that we would have been detained against our wills.[17] But nonetheless he drew us from the palace one day by saying that for the good of the citizens he wanted to hold a general assembly at Santa Maria Novella outside the city and that he would like the *signoria* to be there. Because refusing to go would have seemed too suspicious, we decided that three of us would go while the others remained in the palace.

Messer Charles had his people armed and stationed them inside and outside the gates to guard the city: false counselors had told him that he would not be able to return inside and that the gates would be closed against him. Under this pretext he had wickedly planned—if the entire *signoria* had gone there—to kill us outside the gate and assail the city for the Black Party. And this did not come about because only three Priors went there. He said nothing to them, acting like someone who had no desire to talk, but only to kill.

16. The new *signori* were elected by the *signori* then in office, together with the Captains of the Guilds and certain leading *popolani*.

17. The law required the *signori* to live, eat, and sleep in the recently-constructed Palazzo della Signoria; even returning home to sleep was tantamount to resigning from office.

Many citizens mourned for us at that excursion, thinking that those who went were going to their martyrdom. And when they returned, the citizens praised God for having rescued them from death.

The *signori* were harried from all sides. Good men told them to look out for themselves and their city. The wicked harassed them with questions, and the day went by in questions and answers. Messer Charles's barons kept them busy with long speeches. And so they lived with trouble.

One day a holy man came to us hooded and in secret; he begged us not to reveal his name. He said: "Lords, great tribulation is coming upon you and your city. Ask the bishop to stage a procession, and stipulate to him that it not go across the Arno, and a great part of the danger will cease." This was a man of holy life and great abstinence and good reputation, named Friar Benedetto. We followed his advice, though many sneered at us, saying that it was better to sharpen the swords. In the councils we passed harsh and strong laws and gave the magistrates authority against whoever might start a brawl or tumult; we imposed penalties against persons and had the axe and block set in the piazza to punish evildoers and lawbreakers.

We increased the authority of messer Schiatta Cancellieri, the war captain, and urged him to do good; but nothing worked, because his messengers, servants, and guards betrayed him. The Priors discovered that twenty of their guards had been offered a thousand florins to kill them; they expelled these men from the palace. The Priors strove hard to defend the city from the malice of their adversaries, but nothing worked because they used peaceful means when they should have been strong and violent. Decency is of no avail against great malice.

14 The citizens of the Black Party spoke openly, saying: "We have the lord in our house; the pope is our protector. Our adversaries are not prepared for war or peace. They have no money; the soldiers are not paid." They had put in order everything needed for war so as to receive all their allies in the Oltrarno neighborhood; they arranged to assemble there men from Siena, Perugia, Lucca, San Miniato, Volterra, and San Gimignano. They had subverted all the neighborhood associations, and they had laid plans to hold the bridge of Santa Trinità and set up on two palaces some engines to throw stones. And they had summoned many men from the surrounding villages and all those exiled from Florence.

The White Guelfs were not eager to gather armed men in their homes, for the Priors threatened to punish whoever assembled a troop and so intimidated both friends and enemies. However, friends should not have believed that their own friends would have put them to death for trying to save their city, despite the ordinance. But the White Guelfs let things go, less out of fear of the law than out of stinginess, because messer Torrigiano de' Cerchi was told: "Get yourself ready, and tell this to your friends."

15 The Blacks, recognizing that their enemies were timid and had lost their vigor, hastened to seize the city. One Saturday, November [4], they armed themselves and their horses and began to follow the arranged plan.[18] After vespers that day the Medici, powerful *popolani*, attacked and wounded a brave *popolano* named Orlanduccio Orlandi and left him for dead. The people armed themselves, on foot and horse, and came to the palace of the Priors. And one valiant citizen named Catellina Raffacani said: "Lords, you have been betrayed. Night is coming; don't delay. Send for the rural militia, and tomorrow at dawn strike against your adversaries."

The podestà did not send his servants to the evildoer's house nor did the Standard-bearer of Justice move to punish his misdeed, because he had ten days' grace.

The rural militia was summoned. They came and displayed their banners, and then secretly went over to the Black Party and did not present themselves to serve the commune. There was no one willing to urge the people to assemble at the palace of the Priors, even though the banner of justice was at the windows. Those soldiers who had not been corrupted gathered there, along with other people; and these men, being at the palace in arms, drew something of a following. Some other friendly citizens assembled there on foot and horse, and some enemies, to see what would come of things.

The *signori* were not accustomed to war, and they were kept busy by many who wanted to be heard; and soon night fell. The podestà did not send his servants or arm himself: he left the Priors to do his job which empowered him to go to an evildoer's house with arms, with fire, and with swords. The assembled people came to no decision. The captain, messer Schiatta Cancellieri, did not come forward to take action to oppose the foe, for he was a man better suited to peace and repose than to war. Even though it was widely said that he boasted he would kill messer Charles, this was not true.

When night came the people began to leave. They fortified their houses, and barricaded the streets with wood so that people could not race through them.

18. The date is left blank in the manuscripts. Perhaps Compagni remembered that the turmoil started on the first Saturday of November, but was balked by his error in dating Charles' entrance into Florence (above, II, 9).

16 Messer Manetto Scali (in whom the White Party had great faith since he was strong in friends and followers) began to fortify his palace and set up engines to throw stones. The Spini had their great palace opposite his and they had made it strong; they knew well that they would have to take refuge there from the great force that was expected from the Scali household.

At this time the factions began to employ a new wickedness as they exchanged friendly words. The Spini said to the Scali: "Come, why are we acting like this? After all, we are friends and kinsmen, and all Guelfs. Our only intention is to remove from our necks the chain by which the *popolo* holds both you and us, and then we will be greater than we are now. Have mercy, for God's sake: let us be united, as we should be." And the Buondelmonti spoke like this to the Gherardini, the Bardi to the Mozzi, and messer Rosso della Tosa to Baschiera his kinsman; and many others did the same. Those who listened to these words let their hearts be softened by love of the Guelf Party, and their followers became timid. This convinced the Ghibellines that they had been tricked and betrayed by those in whom they trusted, and they were left all bewildered. Few people were left on the streets except some artisans who had been entrusted with guard duty.

17 Messer Charles's barons and that wicked knight messer Muciatto Franzesi always stayed near the *signori*, saying that they should be allowed to guard the city and the gates and especially the Oltrarno neighborhood. They said that guarding that neighborhood was the responsibility of their lord, and that he wanted to execute harsh justice on evildoers. And under this cover they were hiding their wickedness: they did this to acquire more jurisdiction over the city.

They were not given the keys, but the gates of the Oltrarno were handed over to them: the Florentine guards were removed and Frenchmen put in their place. And in my hands (I, Dino, receiving the oath on behalf of the commune), messer Guglielmo the chancellor and messer Charles's marshal swore and pledged their lord's word that he would take upon himself the protection of the city and guard it and keep it at the request of our *signoria*. And I never believed that such a lord, of the royal house of France, would break his word. But only a small part of the following night had passed before he let Gherarduccio Buondelmonti, who had been banished, enter through the gate we had entrusted to his guard, together with many other exiles.

The *signori* were petitioned by a brave *popolano* named Aglione di Giova

Aglioni, who said: "Lords, it would be wise to have the gate of San Pancrazio closed more securely." They told him to have it fortified as he wished, and sent the master craftsmen there with their banner. The Tornaquinci, a powerful clan with many friends and men-at-arms, attacked and wounded these master craftsmen and put them to flight; and some footsoldiers who were in the guard towers abandoned their posts in fear. From this and from another piece of news, the Priors saw that there was no remedy. They learned the other from a man who was captured one night, a man who went around visiting the powerful households in the guise of a spice seller, telling them that they should arm themselves before daybreak. And so all the Priors' hopes perished, and they decided to defend themselves as soon as the village militia arrived to support them. But this plan failed, because the wicked villagers abandoned them and hid their banners, removing them from their poles. The Priors' servants betrayed them; the gentlemen of Lucca, having been plundered by the Bordoni and deprived of the houses where they were living, broke faith and left; and many soldiers turned coat to serve their enemies. The podestà did not take arms, but with his words went around gathering support for messer Charles of Valois.

18   The following day [19] messer Charles's barons, messer Cante da Gubbio, and many others hounded the Priors, occupying their time and deliberations with long speeches. They swore that their lord felt he had been betrayed and that he was calling his knights to arms, and that his vengeance would be as great as they wished. They said: "Rest assured that if our lord does not have the heart to avenge this misdeed to your liking, you can chop off our heads." The podestà said the same thing: he had come from the house of messer Charles and had heard him swear with his own mouth that he would hang messer Corso Donati. Messer Corso, though banished, had come from Ugnano and entered Florence that morning with twelve companions. He crossed the Arno and went along the wall to San Piero Maggiore, which was not guarded by his foes, and he entered the city like a brave and bold knight. What messer Charles had sworn was not the truth, for messer Corso had come with his knowledge.

After messer Corso had entered Florence, the Whites were informed of his coming and went against him with what forces they could muster. But those who were well horsed were not eager to oppose him, and the others,

---

19. November 6, the day after the attack of the Tornaquinci on the craftsmen and the return of Corso Donati (which Compagni is about to recount).

seeing themselves abandoned, pulled back.[20] Messer Corso took the houses of the Corbizzi at San Piero Maggiore without hindrance and planted his banners there. He broke open the prisons so that the prisoners escaped, and many people followed him in a large force. The Cerchi took refuge in their houses, keeping the doors closed.

The agents of all this evil worked fraudulently; they induced messer Schiatta Cancellieri and messer Lapo Salterelli to come to the Priors and say: "Lords, you can see that messer Charles is very upset. He wants the vengeance to be harsh and the Commune to remain in control. And therefore we think that both parties should choose their most powerful men and place them in his custody. And then the greatest vengeance can be exacted."

These words were far from the truth. Messer Lapo drew up the lists; messer Schiatta ordered all those whose names were listed to go to messer Charles, all for the greater calm of the city. The Blacks went there with confidence, the Whites with fear. Messer Charles had them guarded: he let the Blacks go, but kept the Whites prisoners that night, without straw or mattresses, like murderers.

Oh good King Louis who was so God-fearing, where is the good faith of the royal house of France, now brought low by bad counsel, not fearing dishonor?[21] Oh wicked counselors, you have made the offspring of such high royalty not a soldier but an assassin, one who imprisons citizens wrongly, breaks faith, and belies the name of the royal house of France! Maestro Ruggieri, a sworn follower of that house, told messer Charles when he came to his convent: "A noble city is dying under you." Messer Charles replied that he knew nothing about it.

19 With the leaders of the White Party detained like this, people were dismayed and began to lament. The Priors ordered that the great bell on their palace be rung, but it accomplished nothing because the people were too dismayed to assemble. Not a single armed man, on horse or foot, came forth from the Cerchi household. Only messer Goccia and messer Bindo Adimari with their brothers and sons came to the palace; and since no one else came, they returned to their homes, leaving the piazza deserted.

That evening a miraculous sign appeared in the sky: a vermilion cross over the palace of the Priors. Each bar was more than a palm and a half

20. The magnates fought on horseback, the *popolani* on foot. The magnates, some of whom sympathized with Corso Donati, were reluctant to contest his return.

21. Compagni invokes the memory of the saintly Louis IX of France as a foil to the shameful treachery of his descendent, Charles of Valois.

wide; one line appeared to be more than forty feet high, and the transverse was a little less. This cross remained for as long as it takes a horse to run two laps. The people who saw this—and I saw it clearly—could understand that God was firmly set against our tormented city.

The men who feared their foes hid themselves in their friends' houses. One enemy attacked the other: houses were set afire, robberies were committed, and belongings fled from the homes of the powerless. The powerful Blacks extorted money from the Whites; they married young girls by force; they killed men. And when a house blazed, messer Charles asked: "What is that fire?" He was told that it was a hut, but it was a rich palace. And this evildoing lasted six days, for that was how it had been arranged. The countryside was in flames on every side.

The Priors saw this evildoing multiply, and out of compassion for the city they asked many powerful *popolani* to show mercy, begging them for God's sake to have compassion for their city; but they would do nothing. And therefore the Priors resigned their office.[22]

The new Priors took office on November 8, 1301. They were Baldo Ridolfi, Duccio di Gherardino Magalotti, Neri di messer Iacopo Ardinghelli, Ammannato di Rota Beccannugi, messer Andrea da Cerreto, Ricco di ser Compagno degli Albizzi, and Tedice Manovelli, Standard-bearer of Justice— all *popolani* of the worst sort, and powerful in their party. They passed a law forbidding the old Priors from gathering together in any place, on peril of decapitation. And when the six days set aside for pillaging were done, they selected as podestà messer Cante Gabrielli da Gubbio, who redressed many evils and many charges, and also let many go.[23]

20   A knight in the mold of Catiline the Roman, but more cruel; noble of blood, handsome of body, a charming speaker, adorned with good breeding, subtle of intellect, with his mind always set on evildoing; one who gathered many armed men and kept a great entourage, who ordered many arsons and robberies and did great damage to the Cerchi and their friends,

22. These Priors were supposed to remain in office until December 15, but the city had clearly slipped from their control. On November 7 they announced the names of the new Priors, all members of the Black party, and on the following day they resigned.

23. The Blacks had decided, with the connivance of Charles of Valois, to leave the city in anarchy for several days, giving themselves an opportunity to pursue their vendettas. The office of podestà, the highest judicial office in the city, was left vacant for those days. At the end of this period of anarchy, messer Cante was named podestà, order was restored, and amends were made for some of the worst excesses.

who gained many possessions and rose to great heights: such was messer Corso Donati, who because of his pride was called the Baron. When he passed through the city many cried "long live the Baron," and the city seemed to belong to him. He was led by vanity, and bestowed many favors.

The time had come for messer Charles of Valois, a lord given to lavish and uncontrolled spending, to reveal his wicked intentions, and so he began to try to extort money from the citizens. He summoned the old Priors, whom he had honored and invited to dinner, and to whom he had promised on his faith and in his sealed letters that he would not attack the officials of the city nor contravene the municipal laws. He tried to extort money from them, charging that they had denied him free passage, taken away his office of peacemaker, harmed the Guelf Party, and started building fortifications at Poggibonsi, an affront to his honor and that of the king of France. He persecuted them in this manner to get money. Baldo Ridolfi, one of the new Priors, was his go-between; he said: "You would rather give him your money than go off to Apulia as prisoners." They gave him nothing, because disapproval grew so strong throughout the city that he let matters drop.

In Florence there was a rich *popolano* and very good man named Rinuccio di Senno Rinucci, who had received messer Charles very honorably at a nice place he owned, when he went hawking with his barons. Messer Charles had him arrested and demanded a ransom of four thousand florins, or else he would send him to Apulia as a prisoner. However, at the prayers of his friends, he released him for eight hundred florins. And messer Charles collected a lot of money by such means.

The Donati, Rossi, Tornaquinci, and Bostichi did terrible evils; they violated and robbed many people. The sons of Corteccione Bostichi, in particular, undertook to protect the goods of a friend of theirs, a rich *popolano* named Geri Rossoni, and they received a hundred florins from him for protecting him; and after they were paid, they robbed him. When Geri complained about this, their father offered him as much of his own land as would satisfy him; and he wanted to give Geri a farm he had at San Sepolcro which was worth more than what his sons had taken. And because he wanted the difference in cash, Geri replied to him: "So you want me to pay you for having your sons take my land? I have no wish to do this for it would be poor compensation." And so the matter rested.

These Bostichi did many evil deeds, and they persisted in doing them. They tortured men in their houses, which were in the middle of the city by the New Market, and they put them to the torment in broad daylight.

Throughout the city it was commonly said: "There are many tribunals." And enumerating the places where torture was used it was said: "In the Bostichi house, by the market."

21 Many wicked sins were committed against virgin women; children were robbed; helpless men were despoiled of their goods and driven from their city. The victors passed many ordinances—whatever they wanted, however many, and in whatever form. Many men were accused, and they were induced to confess to conspiracy even though they had done nothing, and they were fined a thousand florins each. Whoever did not come to defend himself was charged nonetheless, and his goods were confiscated and he himself condemned as contumacious. Those who obeyed the summons, payed the fine; and then, accused of new crimes, they were expelled from Florence without the slightest compassion.

Many fortunes were hidden in secret places; many people changed their tune from one day to the next. Many villainous and unjust things were said against the old Priors, even by those who a short time before had praised them. They were greatly slandered to please their adversaries and suffered much ill treatment. Those who spoke badly of them were lying, because the old Priors were entirely dedicated to the common good and the well-being of the republic. But it was useless to contest this because their foes were full of confidence: God favored them; the pope helped them; they had messer Charles as their champion; they did not fear any enemies. The Cerchi, because of their fear and greed, made no preparations—and they were the leaders in this discord. So as not to feed troops, and out of cowardice, they prepared no defense and no refuge for their exile. When they were blamed or reproved for this, they replied that they feared the laws. And this was not true: when messer Torrigiano de' Cerchi came to the *signori* to know where he stood, in my presence he was advised to prepare himself and get ready to defend himself, and to tell this to his other friends, and to act like a brave man. The Cerchi did not do this; because of their cowardice, they lacked the heart. As a result their adversaries took courage and rose up. And so the Priors gave the keys of the city to messer Charles.

22 O wicked citizens, authors of your city's destruction, you have brought this upon it! And you, Ammannato di Rota Beccannugi, disloyal citizen, who viciously turned on the Priors and with threats plied them to give you the keys: look where your malicious deeds have brought us!

O you, Donato Alberti, who made the citizens live with trouble, where is your arrogance—you who hid yourself in Nuto Marignolli's humble kitchen? And you, Nuto, elder and leader of your neighborhood, who in your loyalty to the Guelf Party let yourself be deceived?

O messer Rosso della Tosa, fulfill your great desire: you who in your craving for lordship laid claim to the large share and excluded your brothers from their portion.

O messer Geri Spini, fulfill your desire: uproot the Cerchi, so that you can live securely in your felonies.

O messer Lapo Salterelli, who threatened and beat the magistrates who did not take your side in your disputes, where did you arm yourself? In the Pulci house, keeping well hidden.

O messer Berto Frescobaldi, who acted like such a friend of the Cerchi and made yourself a mediator in this dispute to get from them twelve thousand florins in loan, how did you earn those florins? Where did you show yourself?

O messer Manetto Scali, who wanted to be thought so great and to be so feared, believing that you would always remain lord, where did you take arms? Where is your following? Where are the mail-clad horses? You let yourself submit to those who were not at all feared in comparison with you.

O you, *popolani*, who craved office and sucked the honors and occupied the palaces of the magistrates, where was your defense? In lies, simulating and dissimulating, blaming your friends and praising your enemies, merely to save yourselves. Weep, therefore, for yourselves and your city.

23 Many who had formerly been unknown became great through wicked deeds. Ruling with cruelty, they exiled many citizens and made them into rebels and condemned them in their goods and their persons. They laid waste many great houses and punished many, as they had agreed in writing among themselves. No one escaped without being punished: kinship and friendship were worth nothing, nor could the predetermined penalties be reduced or changed. New marriages were worth nothing; every friend became an enemy. Brother abandoned brother, son abandoned father. Every affection, all humanity was extinguished. They sent many into exile sixty miles from the city. They laid on them many heavy burdens and taxes and took from them great sums; many fortunes were destroyed. No accord, pity, or mercy was to be found in anyone. The greatest man was he who cried loudest: "Death, death to the traitors."

Many long-standing members of the White Party and old Ghibellines were received as partners by the Blacks, merely because of their evildoing.

Among these were messer Betto Brunelleschi, messer Giovanni Rustichelli, messer Baldo Aguglioni, messer Fazio da Signa, and many others who dedicated themselves to destroying the Whites. Messer Andrea and messer Aldobrandino da Cerreto, who today call themselves Cerretani, surpassed all the others: they were of ancient Ghibelline origin, and became Black Guelfs.

24 Baschiera della Tosa was the young son of a Party member—a knight named messer Bindo del Baschiera who suffered many persecutions for the Guelf Party, lost an eye to an arrow at the castle of Fucecchio, and was wounded and killed in the battle with the Aretines.[24] This Baschiera survived his father. He should have held offices in the city since he was a young man who deserved them; but he was deprived of them because the elders of his house took the offices and their income for themselves and did not share them. He was an ardent supporter of the Guelf Party; when the city turned around at messer Charles's arrival, he vigorously armed himself and fought his kinsmen and adversaries with fire and sword, with the troop of infantry he had with him.

The Romagnole infantry which the commune had hired, seeing that the city would be lost, abandoned Baschiera and went to the palace to collect their pay. They asked for it in order to have an excuse to leave; but the Priors begged a hundred florins from Baldone Angelotti and gave them to the troops. This man who lent them the money wanted the infantry to stay with him to guard his house, and so Baschiera lost the troops he had led. If the other citizens of his party had matched his vigor, they would not have lost! But they cherished foolish hopes, letting themselves believe that they would not be harmed.

25 After messer Charles had reestablished the Black Party in Florence, he went to Rome. He asked for money from the pope, who replied that he had put him in the fountain of gold.[25]

A few days after this it was reported that some of the White Party were plotting with messer Piero Ferrante of Languedoc, one of messer Charles's barons, and written agreements were discovered according to which he was to kill messer Charles at their instigation.[26] Messer Charles, who had returned to Florence from the Papal Court, called a secret council of seventeen

24. At Campaldino: see above, I, 10.
25. Charles of Valois left for Rome on February 13, 1302, and returned to Florence on March 18.
26. Eight days after the return of Charles of Valois, a written pact was discovered which linked Baschiera della Tosa, Baldinaccio Adimari, and Naldo Gherardini in a con-

citizens one night. In this council they planned to seize certain men, declare them guilty, and have their heads cut off. This council was reduced to a smaller number when seven of them left the other ten behind; they did this to warn the men in question to flee and leave the city.

That night messer Goccia Adimari and his son fled secretly; and messer Manetto Scali left Calenzano and went farther away, to Mangona.[27] Not long afterward messer Muccio da Biserno, a mercenary with a large troop, and messer Simone Cancellieri, an enemy of messer Manetto, arrived at Calenzano expecting to find him there; and in searching for him they even poked through the straw mattresses with their swords.

The following day messer Charles had messer Manetto and many others summoned, condemned them as contumacious and as traitors, and burned their houses and confiscated their goods on behalf of the commune, by right of his office as peacemaker. Messer Manetto had his partners ransom those goods for five thousand florins, so that the books of his French company would not be taken from him; and they protected themselves with that company.

Messer Giano di messer Vieri de' Cerchi, a young knight, was summoned to the palace of messer Charles and placed in the guard of two French knights who detained him politely in the house.[28] Messer Paniccia degli Erri and messer Berto Frescobaldi, hearing of this, went to the palace (which belonged to them) and placed themselves between messer Giano and the two guards, talking to them. They signaled to him to leave and so he slipped away. It was said that messer Charles would first have robbed him of lots of money and then his life. Similar things happened to many of those summoned who had already left: messer Charles condemned them in their goods and their persons, and confiscated their goods for the commune. As a result he received from the commune twenty-four thousand florins; and he declared himself paid in full for all he had done for them under the title of peacemaker.

In the month of April 1302, having summoned many Ghibelline citizens and Guelfs of the White Party, he condemned the Uberti, the family of the Scolari, the Lamberti, degli Abati, Soldanieri, Rinaldeschi, Migliorelli, and Tebaldini. He banished and confined the whole family of the Cerchi; messer

spiracy to kill him. But even Giovanni Villani, a partisan of the Black Guelfs, believed that this document was forged by the Blacks as an excuse to take further action against their rivals.

27. Calenzano is a village just eight miles from Florence, in the direction of Prato. Mangona is about twenty miles from Florence.

28. Messer Giano had distinguished himself at the battle of Campaldino; see I, 10.

Baldo, messer Biligiardo, Baldo di messer Talano, and Baschiera della Tosa; messer Goccia and his son, Corso di messer Forese, and Baldinaccio Adimari; messer Vanni de' Mozzi; messer Manetto and Vieri Scali; Naldo Gherardini; the counts of Gangalandi; messer Neri da Gaville; messer Lapo Salterelli; messer Donato di messer Alberto Ristori; Orlanduccio Orlandi; Dante Alighieri, who was ambassador at Rome; the sons of Lapo Arrighi; the Ruffoli; the Angelotti; the Amuniti, Lapo del Biondo and his sons; Giovangiacotto Malispini; the Tedaldi; Corazza Ubaldini; ser Petracca di ser Parenzo dall'Incisa, notary of the *Riformazioni*; [29] Masino Cavalcanti and some of his relatives; messer Betto Gherardini; Donato and Teghia Finiguerri; Nuccio Galligai and Tignoso de' Macci; and many others. There were more than six hundred men, who went here and there through the world.

26 The city was left under the rule of messer Corso Donati, messer Rosso della Tosa, messer Pazzino de' Pazzi, messer Geri Spini, messer Betto Brunelleschi, the Buondelmonti, the Agli, the Tornaquinci, some of the Gianfigliazzi, the Bardi, some of the Frescobaldi, the Rossi, some of the Nerli, the Pulci, the Bostichi, the Magalotti, the Manieri, the Bisdomini, the Uccellini, the Bordoni, the Strozzi, the Rucellai, the Acciaiuoli, the Altoviti, the Aldobrandini, the Peruzzi and the Monaldi, Borgo Rinaldi and his brother, Palla Anselmi, Manno Attaviani, Nero Cambi, Noffo Guidi, Simone Gherardi, Lapo Guazza, and many others from the city and the countryside. None of them can deny that he was a destroyer of the city. Nor can they say that any need constrained them, other than pride and competition for offices. For the enmity between citizens was not so great that it would have embroiled the city in war, if the false *popolani* had not had minds corrupted to do evil, to profit or rather to rob, and to hold the offices of the city.

One young man named Bertuccio de' Pulci, returning from France and finding his partners banished from the city, left his relatives in the government and joined his partners in exile. And he did this out of great spirit.

27 The captain messer Schiatta Cancellieri (from whose house the two damned parties of Guelfs arose in Florence) returned to Pistoia and began to arm and provision his castles, especially Montale in the direction of Florence and Serravalle in the direction of Lucca. The Black Party of Florence immediately went to messer Charles of Valois, urging him to conquer Pistoia and promising to give him much money. For this purpose they had him ride

29. This ser Petracca, who had been the public employee charged with recording the decisions of the communal councils, was the father of the poet Francesco Petrarch.

there with his troops, in rather bad order. The city was strong and fortified with a good wall, deep ditches, and brave citizens. Messer Charles was led there several times, so that Mainardo da Susinana reproved him and said that he was foolish to go. As a result of this bad guidance he and his troops were led into the marshes in rainy weather, and the Pistoiese could easily have captured him there if they had so desired. But they feared his greatness, and let him escape.

The Florentines and Lucchese laid siege to Serravalle. They knew that it was not provisioned because messer Schiatta, talking with messer Geri Spini and messer Pazzino de' Pazzi, who were wiser than he, told them it was not. The castle therefore surrendered on terms which guaranteed the safety of the defenders; these terms were not kept, and the Pistoiese were taken captive.

As a result of negotiations between the garrison of Montale and messer Pazzino de' Pazzi (who lived nearby, at Palugiano), that castle was given to the Florentines for three thousand florins and torn down.

28 Messer Charles of Valois left for Apulia to conduct the war over Sicily.[30] Once he had gone, the Blacks of Florence—preferring to ruin the city rather than lose their rule—started to destroy their adversaries in every way.

The Whites went to Arezzo, where the podestà was Uguccione della Faggiuola, an old Ghibelline who had risen from humble origins. This man was corrupted by the vain hope that Pope Boniface would make his son a cardinal, and at the pope's request he treated the Whites so badly that they had to leave. A good part of them went to Forlì, where the vicar for the Church was Scarpetta degli Ordelaffi, a nobleman from Forlì.

Many horrible misfortunes befell the White and Ghibelline Party. They had a castle in the Valdarno at Pian di Sco, which was held by Carlino de' Pazzi with sixty horse and many footsoldiers. The Blacks of Florence laid siege to it. It was said that Carlino betrayed the Whites for cash in hand.[31] By this means the Blacks got their troops inside and captured the men; they killed some and let the rest be ransomed. Among others, they let a son of messer Donato di messer Alberto Ristori, named Alberto, be ransomed for

30. Charles left Tuscany in early April to fulfill his original purpose in coming to Italy: to fight the Aragonese for the possession of Sicily. His campaign was a failure and early in 1303 he returned to France, where he died in 1325. According to Giovanni Villani (VIII, 50), people said of Charles that he came to Tuscany as a peacemaker and left the land in war; he went to Sicily to wage war and brought back a shameful peace.

31. Giovanni Villani (VIII, 53) confirms this treason of Carlino de' Pazzi.

three thousand lire. And they hanged two of the Scolari, two Bogolesi, one of the Lamberti, one of the Migliorelli, and some others.

The Ghibellines and Whites who had taken refuge in Siena did not feel safe staying there, for there was a prophecy which said: "The she-wolf is a whore." That is, Siena (which is represented by the she-wolf) gave them license to stay one moment and took it away the next. And therefore they decided not to remain there.

29 With the aid of the Ubaldini, the Whites and Ghibellines opened war in the Mugello. But first the Ubaldini wanted to be insured against damages. They were offered surety by the Pisans, but the Pisan Vannuccio Bonconti had been bribed to favor the Black Party and so they got no help or support from him.

Messer Tolosato degli Uberti heard of this discord, returned from Sardinia, aligned himself with the Pisans in support of the Ghibelline party, and went in person to Bologna and Pistoia. He was joined by many others of the Uberti house. For more than forty years they had been rebels against their country, and found neither mercy nor peace. Even in exile they kept great state and never diminished their honor, for they always associated with kings and lords and dedicated themselves to great undertakings.

The Black Party crossed the Apennines and burned villages and towns. They entered the Garden of the Ubaldini in the Santerno valley, and burned it. And no one took arms in its defense! If someone had just cut down some trees there and laid them on the ground to obstruct the narrow passes, not one of their enemies could have escaped.

The Whites suffered another misfortune thanks to the stupidity of a rebel citizen of Florence named Gherardino Diedati, who was staying in Pisa. Confiding in his relatives, he wrote them that the exiles hoped to return to Florence by force from one month to the next; and he wrote the same thing to some of his friends. His letters were discovered and as a result two young nephews of his, sons of Finiguerra Diedati, were arrested and their heads cut off, along with Masino Cavalcanti, a fine young man. Tignoso de' Macci was put to torture and died of it, and one of the Gherardini had his head cut off.[32] Oh, how the sorrowful mother of those two boys was deceived! With overflowing tears, all disheveled, kneeling in the middle of the street, she threw herself on the ground in front of the jurist messer Andrea da Cerreto, with her arms crossed begging him for God's sake to try to save

32. The bodies of those who were executed and of those who died in the course of this investigation were buried on January 25, 1303.

her sons. He replied that he was going to the palace for that very reason—and he was a liar, because he was going there to put them to death. Those citizens who had hoped that the city could be pacified lost their hope because of these evil deeds: until that day no blood had been shed which would have prevented peace in the city.[33]

30   The third misfortune befell the Whites and Ghibellines (and thereby brought them together, and reduced the two names to a single one) in this way. When Folcieri da Calboli was podestà in Florence, the Whites selected as their captain Scarpetta degli Ordelaffi, a temperate young man and an enemy of Folcieri. They gathered a great force under his command and came to Pulicciano near Borgo San Lorenzo, hoping to be able to use Monte Accenico, built with three circuits of walls by the cardinal messer Ottaviano degli Ubaldini. There they swelled their numbers with their friends, believing that they could take Pulicciano and then advance on the city. Folcieri rode there with a few horsemen. The Blacks approached very cautiously; then, seeing that their enemies did not attack the podestà and his small troop but instead cut the bridges and assumed a defensive position, they took heart as they increased in number. The Whites feared that they would be trapped, and so they retired in disorder. Whoever was not quick to escape, was caught there; the peasants of the counts in that area immediately occupied the passes, and captured and killed many of them.

Scarpetta and many of the other leaders took refuge in Monte Accenico. The army of the Whites and Ghibellines included seven hundred horse and four thousand footsoldiers. And although their retreat was not honorable, it was wiser than their advance.

Messer Donato Alberti fled so slowly that he was captured, as were a valiant youth named Nerlo di messer Goccia Adimari and two young Scolari. And Nanni Ruffoli was killed by Chirico di messer Pepo della Tosa.

Messer Donato was led before the podestà mounted shamefully on an ass and dressed in a peasant's tunic. When the podestà saw him, he asked: "You are messer Donato Alberti?" He replied: "I am Donato. But it is Andrea da Cerreto, Nicola Acciaiuoli, Baldo Aguglioni, and Iacopo da Certaldo who should appear before you, for it is they who have destroyed Florence."[34]

Then they put him to the torture, and fastened the rope on the winch and

---

33. Until this time only Ghibellines had been sentenced to death; White Guelfs had suffered only exile, fines, or the confiscation of their goods. These executions ended any hope of reconciliation between the Guelf factions.

34. Messer Donato, a well-known lawyer, singles out the prominent lawyers among the Blacks.

let him hang there. They opened the windows and doors of the palace, and summoned many other citizens on various pretexts so that they might see his torment and the mockery they made of him. And the podestà worked it so that he was allowed to cut off messer Donato's head. He did this because war was good for him and peace harmful; and he did this with all of the captives. This was not a just decision: it was against both the communal laws, which said that exiled citizens who wanted to return to their homes should not be condemned to death, and the customs of war, which said that they should be held captive. And because the captured White Guelfs were killed just like the Ghibellines, they became sure of one another; for up to that day each had always doubted that the others were with them wholeheartedly.

31 O messer Donato, how fortune turned against you! First they captured your son, whom you ransomed for three thousand lire, and then they decapitated you. Who did this to you? The Guelfs, whom you loved so much that in your every speech you said a whole column against the Ghibellines. How could the name of Guelf be taken from you by these false reports? How could the Guelfs execute you among the Ghibellines? Who took the name of Guelf from Baldinaccio Adimari and Baschiera della Tosa, whose fathers did so much for the Guelf Party? Who had the authority to take and give in an instant, so that Ghibellines were called Guelfs and the great Guelfs called Ghibellines? Who had this privilege? Messer Rosso della Tosa and his followers, who did nothing for the needs of the Party, nothing at all by comparison with the fathers of those from whom this name was stripped. And therefore that wise and very Guelf man Corazza Ubaldini da Signa spoke well when, seeing the Blacks force men to become Ghibellines, he said: "There are so many who are Ghibelline by choice, that it is not good to create more of them by force."

32 The boldness of the Blacks grew so great that they allied themselves with the marquis of Ferrara to seize Bologna and rode there with six hundred horse and six thousand footsoldiers. And one of the two parties within the city, which were both Guelf, was supposed to attack the other on Easter Day.

The Whites who had taken refuge in Bologna armed themselves manfully and held a muster. The Blacks were intimidated and did not attack. The marquis disbanded his army and the Blacks left. Because of this, the situation of the Whites improved in Bologna and henceforth they were welcomed there and the Blacks were considered enemies. The Bolognese made league with the Romagnoles; they argued that the marquis had tried to betray them, and that if he had accomplished this he would have thrown the Romagna into confusion. This league included Forlì and Faenza, Bernardino da Polenta, the White Party of Florence, the Pistoiese, count Federigo da Montefeltro, and the Pisans. In the month of June 1303, the members of the league raised a levy of five hundred horse and made messer Salinguerra of Ferrara their captain.[35]

33 The Whites rode from Monte Accenico to the area of Lastra, burning whatever they found.

The Aretines recaptured Castiglione and Monte San Savino and laid waste to Laterina, which was held by the Blacks. The Blacks could not succor it because they were with the Lucchese around Pisa. But when they heard of this attack, the Blacks left the Lucchese on guard in Florence and rode to Montevarchi with the knights of the marquis, to succor Laterina.

The Aretines joined with the Whites, with their allies from the Romagna, and with Pisan soldiers, and they rode to Castiglione degli Ubertini. They thought this would give notice that battle was drawn. But the Blacks left there and attacked Castiglione Aretino, where they lost some footsoldiers; they then reinforced Montalcino and Laterina.

The Whites had twelve hundred horse and plenty of infantry, and they appeared ready to fight with great vigor. But they were deceived by certain traitors who took money from their enemies: these traitors spoke against giving battle (which could certainly have been won), claiming that the Pisans did not want to take a chance on combat.

Uguccione della Faggiuola was in Arezzo, as I said. He was removed from the *signoria* because of some suspicious behavior, and his office was given instead to count Federigo, son of the good count Guido da Montefeltro whose noble reputation spread all over the world. He came to Arezzo and assumed the government, accompanied by Ciappettino Ubertini.

34 The Blacks returned to Florence, and within a short time discord arose among them because messer Rosso della Tosa, messer Pazzino de' Pazzi, and messer Geri Spini, with the support of the *popolo grasso*, held the lordship and offices of the city. Messer Corso Donati thought that he was more worthy than these men and that he did not have the share which was

35. Salinguerra Torelli, a Ghibelline exile from Ferrara, was an enemy of Azzo VIII Este, marquis of Ferrara.

his due, for he was a most valiant knight in everything he undertook. And so he strove to bring them down, and to undo the Priors who were in office, and to raise himself and his followers. He began to sow discord, and with a pretence of justice and piety he spoke in this fashion: "Poor men are being afflicted with imposts and taxes and despoiled of their property, and some people are filling their purses with it. Let us see where this great sum of money has gone, since it all cannot have been consumed by war." He asked this question very insistently before the *signori* and in the councils. People listened to him willingly; they believed that he spoke in good faith and in any case they wanted an investigation. The other party did not know how to respond since anger and pride held them back. The people did so much with those officials who agreed with them that they saw to it that the attacks, violence, and robberies would be investigated. They called in foreign jurists as auditors. Then the others softened their words; and to foster goodwill the *popolani* in power repatriated those exiles who had observed their bounds, on August 1, 1303.

35 On Saturday, September 7, 1303, Sciarra della Colonna entered Anagni, a city subject to Rome, together with a large troop and the men of Ceccano and a knight who was there on behalf of the king of France, bearing the king's banner and that of the Patrimony, that is, the Keys of Saint Peter. They broke open the sacristy and strongbox of the pope and plundered it of much treasure. The pope, abandoned by his followers, was taken prisoner. It was said that the cardinal messer Francesco Orsini was there in person, along with many Roman citizens. And the king of France was thought to be involved in this plot because the pope was striving to humble him: it was said to be the pope's doing that the Flemish made war on him and brought death to many Frenchmen.[36]

For this reason the king of France assembled in Paris many masters and bachelors of theology, Franciscans and Dominicans and members of many other orders, and there had the pope pronounced a heretic, and then had him reprimanded, charging him with many horrible sins. The pope was captured at Anagni; and without giving any defense or explanation he was led to Rome, where he was wounded in the head and a few days later died enraged.

Many were pleased and delighted by his death, because he ruled cruelly and provoked wars, crushing many people and accumulating much wealth.

36. Flanders had rebelled against King Philip of France in 1302.

The Whites and Ghibellines rejoiced especially, because he was their mortal enemy; but the Blacks grieved over it greatly.

36 In that month of September the Whites and Ghibellines of Florence united under the command of messer Tolosato degli Uberti, a noble Florentine knight and very valiant man of arms. They rode to Arezzo with Pisan soldiers. The Sienese granted them passage, for the citizens of Siena kept on good terms with both parties. When the Whites appeared strong, the Sienese banished them; but the ban was ineffectual because it carried no punishment. They gave help to the Blacks in their sorties and acted like their brothers. And so there was a prophecy about them, which among other words about the Tuscan war said: "The she-wolf is a whore," since the she-wolf is used to represent Siena. The Whites and Ghibellines of Florence, the Romagnoles, the Pisans, and all their other allies gathered at Arezzo, and by the first of November they were in the saddle.

The Blacks rode to Figline, and the Whites descended on Ganghereto. The Aretines went to Laterina and fortified the passes so that no supplies could be brought in. But this castle escaped thanks to hunger and discord among the Aretines, for their leaders secretly took their payment and let Laterina be provisioned.

BOOK III

1 Our Lord God, who provides for all things, wished to restore a good shepherd to the world and provide for the needs of Christians. And so to the throne of St. Peter was elected Pope Benedict, a native of Treviso, prior general of the Dominican Order, a man with few relatives and from an unimportant family, trustworthy and good, discreet and holy. The world rejoiced in new light. Pope Benedict started to do pious deeds; he pardoned the Colonna and restored their goods.[1] On the first fast day he created two cardinals. One was an Englishman. The other was the bishop of Spoleto, a native of the town of Prato, a Dominican named messer Niccolò; he had humble relatives but great learning, and was gracious and wise—but of Ghibelline stock.[2] The Ghibellines and Whites rejoiced greatly over this, and arranged that Pope Benedict send him to Tuscany as peacemaker.

2 Before his arrival, a conspiracy was discovered which had been organized by messer Rosso della Tosa. Everything that this man did and strove for in the city was done so that he might exercise lordship in the manner of the lords of Lombardy.[3] He renounced many profits and made many peace pacts in order to make men ready to do whatever he desired.

Messer Corso Donati did not overlook money. Everyone gave him a share

---

1. He excluded from this pardon Sciarra Colonna, who had attacked Pope Boniface VIII at Anagni (see above, II, 35).

2. Niccolò of Prato was named cardinal-bishop of Ostia and Velletri, but he was generally known as the cardinal of Prato.

3. That is, he wanted to rule Florence as the Visconti ruled Milan, the Este ruled Ferrara, and so on. On the exercise of lordship in the Po valley, see John Larner, *The Lords of Romagna: Romagnol Society and the Origins of the Signorie* (Ithaca: Cornell University Press, 1965).

of his own goods, either out of fear or threats; he did not ask for anything, but gave the impression of wanting it.

These two enemies protected their flanks. Messer Rosso feared the hatred of the Tuscans if he proceeded against messer Corso. He feared enemies from outside the city and he strove to weaken them before revealing his enmity to messer Corso. And he feared that the *popolo* might become unruly because of his standing with the Guelf Party; he sided with the *popolo grasso*, for they were the tongs he used to grasp the hot iron. Messer Corso, because of his great spirit, did not deign to attend to petty things; and because of his scornfulness, he did not retain the affection of such citizens. So he split from the *popolo grasso* and allied himself with the magnates. He pointed out many ways in which they were prisoners and slaves of this populace of *popolani grassi*, or rather dogs, who lorded it over them and appropriated their honors; and with this sort of talk he gathered together all the great citizens who felt oppressed, and they all swore solidarity. They included messer Lottieri della Tosa, bishop of Florence, and his nephew messer Baldo, since his kinsman messer Rossellino had taken possession of one of his castles and its dependents and he had not dared to complain about this as long as Pope Boniface was alive. They also included the Rossi, the Bardi, the Lucardesi, the Cavalcanti, the Bostichi, the Giandonati, almost all of the Tornaquinci, the Manieri, and some of the Adimari, and many *popolani* as well. All told, between great families and *popolani* there were 32 who swore this oath. And they complained about the grain imported from Apulia to feed the *popolo*: "The *popolani* are oppressed and their goods taken by heavy taxes, and then they are left to eat their pallets," meaning that straw was cut into the grain to swell the measure.[4]

The *popolo grasso* began to grow fearful; messer Corso's friends grew stronger—but not too much, because people opposed messer Corso in the councils and assemblies. The Bordoni, who were bold and arrogant *popolani*, attacked him fiercely and opposed him on many occasions, and they did not care whether their adversaries outnumbered them or what might come about in the future. They drew large profits from the commune, and the praise they heard went to their heads. However, the followers of messer Rosso did not let them molest messer Corso. One month they fixed the grain price at twelve *soldi*, and made a new tax estimate, and levied a sub-

4. In years of famine, such as 1303, the commune imported grain and distributed it to those in need. Corso played on the resentment of the *popolo minuto*, who thought the grain was of poor quality and suspected the *signori* and *popolo grasso* of enriching themselves at the expense of poor citizens.

sidy for twelve hundred horses at fifty florins per horse, without any exemptions.[5] And then they sent people to build an outpost near Monte Accenico and placed a garrison there.

3 Since messer Corso's partisans continued to speak openly, the other faction called in the Lucchese. They believed that moderate words would win the strongholds messer Corso held: they set a time within which he was to surrender his strongholds, and condemned him if he would not yield them to the Lucchese.

Messer Corso would not give way to this pressure. He called on his friends and gathered many exiles, and messer Neri da Lucardo, a valiant man at arms, came to his aid. And he came to the piazza armed on horseback and fiercely attacked the palace of the Priors with fire and crossbows.

The other faction, led by messer Rosso della Tosa, together with most of his kinsmen, the Pazzi, the Frescobaldi, the Gherardini, and the Spini, the *popolo*, and many *popolani*, came to the defense of the palace, where there was a great scuffle. In this fight messer Lotteringo Gherardini was killed by an arrow. This was a great loss, for he was a worthy man.

Messer Rosso della Tosa and his followers chose the new group of Priors and installed them in the palace at night, without sound of trumpets or other honors.[6] Barricades were set up throughout the city, and they remained under arms for about a month.

The Lucchese, who had come to Florence to establish peace, were given great authority by the commune.[7] The magnates revealed their desires clearly and asked that the laws against them be revoked. The number of *signori* was doubled, but nonetheless the magnate party remained very proud and bold.

At this time it happened that Testa Tornaquinci and a son of his kinsman Bingieri wounded a *popolano* who was their neighbor and left him for dead in the Old Market. No one was eager to help him, for fear of them. But the *popolo* gathered their courage, worked themselves up, and went to the

5. The rulers of the city tried to appease the populace by fixing the price of grain at a level which (if this passage is correct) was well below the market price. At this time the price of grain normally ranged from twenty to twenty-two *soldi* per *staio*; during this famine it rose to twenty-six *soldi*. They also revised the tax assessments.

6. The old *signori*, who were of messer Rosso's party, chose the new *signori* without the usual ceremony. To strengthen their position, they also doubled the number of *signori*: the Signoria which held office from February 16 to April 16, 1304 consisted of thirteen Priors and the Standard-bearer of Justice, as did the Signoria which followed it.

7. On February 16, 1304, full authority over the city was placed in the hands of sixteen of the Lucchese.

Tornaquinci palace armed with the banner of justice. They set fire to the palace, and burned and destroyed it to punish their arrogance.[8]

4 Cardinal Niccolò of Prato, named Pope Benedict's legate in Tuscany on the secret request of the Whites and Ghibellines of Florence, arrived in Florence on March 10, 1304. The *popolo* of Florence received him very honorably with olive branches and with great rejoicing. After he had rested in Florence for a few days, finding the citizens deeply divided, he asked the *popolo* for authority to constrain the citizens to peace; this was conceded to him until May 1, 1304, and then extended for a year. He made many peace pacts between the citizens living in Florence; but then their ardor cooled and many quibbles were found.

The bishop supported peace because it brought justice and prosperity, and at the cardinal's request he made peace with his kinsman, messer Rosso. The cardinal restored their banners to the militia companies; messer Corso's friends took part in them, and he himself was named Captain of the [Guelf] Party.[9] Everyone supported the cardinal; and with hope [of success] he softened them so with sweet words that they let him name delegates. These delegates were messer Ubertino dello Strozza and ser Bono da Ognano for the [Black] party within the city, and messer Lapo Ricovero and ser Petracca di ser Parenzo dall'Incisa for the [White] party outside it.[10]

On April 26, 1304 the *popolo* gathered in Piazza Santa Maria Novella in the presence of the *signori* and, having made many peace agreements, they kissed one another on the mouth as a sign of peace. They drew up peace contracts and set penalties for whoever contravened them. With olive branches in hand, the Gherardini made peace with the Amieri. Everyone was so pleased with this peacemaking that when a heavy rain fell that day, no one left, and they did not even seem to feel the downpour. Great bonfires were lit; the church bells sounded; everyone rejoiced. But at the palace of the Gianfigliazzi, where great fires were lit for the wars, nothing was done that evening; and the good people talked about this a lot, saying that the Gianfigliazzi did not deserve peace. The companies of the *popolo* went

8. According to the *Cronica marciana magliabechiana* (cited in Del Lungo's edition, II, p. 270), this event took place in April.

9. The cardinal strengthened the *popolo* by reestablishing the nineteen companies of citizen militia which had been founded in 1250. At the same time he tried to satisfy messer Corso by entrusting the command of some of these companies to his followers and by having him named Captain of the Guelf Party.

10. A lawyer and a notary from each party were selected to negotiate the terms of an agreement.

around making a great celebration in the name of the cardinal, bearing the banners which they had received from him in Piazza Santa Croce.

Messer Rosso della Tosa was left very indignant because it seemed to him that these reconciliations had progressed far beyond what he wanted. He therefore thought of pursuing his designs along with the others of his faction, since they let him do as he wished and seemed friendly to him. They did everything possible to take Pistoia, which they feared greatly because their enemies held it and messer Tolosato degli Uberti was there. And meanwhile, the knights and footsoldiers of the Whites were returning to Monte Accenico after relieving Forlì. Because of this, the Guelfs in Florence began to speak dishonestly and disturb the peace. And on top of many other things, they asked the Buondelmonti to make peace with the Uberti: many meetings were held to temporize, for this demand was impossible to meet.

On May 6, 1304 the Priors empowered the cardinal and four men designated by the pope to put the general reconciliation into effect.[11] The four men were messer Martino della Torre of Milan, messer Antonio da Fostierato of Lodi, messer Antonio de' Brusciati of Brescia,[12] and messer Guidotto de' Bugni of Bergamo.

5   Those who were opposed to the pope's will did not wish to tolerate the cardinal's authority any longer, nor let the peace take deeper root. They accomplished so much with their false words that they moved the cardinal to leave Florence, saying to him: "My lord, before you go any further in putting this reconciliation into effect, make certain that Pistoia will obey; because if we make peace and Pistoia remains in our enemies' hands, we will have been tricked." They said this not because they would accept the peace as soon as they had Pistoia, but merely to prolong the peace negotiations. And they so moved the cardinal with their artful words that he set out from Florence on May 8, 1304; and on the road to Campi he lodged at a nice retreat belonging to Rinuccio di Senno Rinucci.

The next day he rode to Prato, his birthplace which he had never revisited. He was received there with much honor and great dignity: there

11. The commune of Florence had asked the pope to name a podestà who would assist the cardinal in making peace between the various factions. In late April the pope replied by naming four Lombard nobles among whom the Florentines could chose. The Florentines then renewed the authority they had earlier conceded to the cardinal, and extended it to include whichever of these Lombard nobles would accept the post. All four, however, declined the offer.

12. The letter of Pope Benedict names instead messer Guglielmotto de' Brusciati of Novara.

were olive branches and knights with silk banners and standards, the people and their ladies well dressed and the streets draped with cloth, dances and instruments, and cries of "Long live the lord." But soon they transformed this honor into shame, just as the Jews did to Christ, as I shall explain.

He rode on to Pistoia that day and spoke to the leading citizens and officials of the city. He was accompanied by messer Geri Spini, who was so sure that he would be granted lordship over Pistoia that he had prepared his insignia of office. They were received very honorably by messer Tolosato degli Uberti and the *popolo*, and the cardinal was given some authority by the *popolo*, but not the authority to give their city to others. He saw from this that the city was ruled very shrewdly and so lost all hope of having it. And so he returned towards Prato, believing that he would be able to enter there on the strength of his relatives and friends; but he could not.[13]

6 Hearing how Prato had been arrayed against him, he left at once and returned to Florence. He condemned and excommunicated the people of Prato and proclaimed a crusade against them, offering remission of sins to whoever did any harm to them. And his relatives and friends were ruined and expelled from Prato.

The podestà of Florence raided the countryside of Prato with the commune's cavalry and hired soldiers. They drew themselves up in the dry bed of the Bisenzio at Olmo a Mezzano, and stayed there until mid-afternoon. Some people came out from Prato to negotiate an agreement with them, apologizing to the cardinal and offering to do whatever he wished, so as to quiet their rage. For there were many who shared the cardinal's desire and would willingly have put them to the sword and tried to conquer their city.

The other leaders of the Black Party and their followers spoke many divisive words.[14] While the knights were drawn up in their ranks, the war was almost settled; but great discord broke out among those people.[15] If the discord had led to open conflict, the magnates and the *popolo*—lovers of peace

13. The Florentines of messer Rosso della Tosa's party, opponents of the peace arrangements, incited their friends in Prato against the cardinal, claiming that he favored the Whites and the Ghibellines. As a result, his relatives and supporters were expelled from Prato.

14. The "other leaders" were those who, like messer Rosso, disagreed with the cardinal.

15. While the army was drawn up near Prato and its presence had nearly intimidated the people of Prato into yielding to the cardinal, discord broke out in Florence between the *popolani grassi*, who opposed the cardinal, and the magnates and *popolo minuto*, who supported him.

and friends of the cardinal—would have had the better of it, judging by the support they received. The men of the Cavalcanti household showed themselves very strongly in their favor.

The army left and went to Campi, where it stayed all that day. It left the next day since the cardinal, believing that he was doing the best for peace, let himself be led by words. But his relatives, who were shamefully expelled, did not return to Prato—they did not dare to—and later they were declared rebels.

7 The cardinal devoted himself to fostering peace and putting it into effect. He was prompted to invite some leaders of the exiles to settle their differences. He chose fourteen of them, who came to Florence with permission and safe-conduct.[16] They stayed across the Arno in the Mozzi household, where they set up wooden barriers and posted guards so that they would not be harmed. Their names were messer [Piggello] de' Conti da Gangalandi, Lapo di messer Azzolino degli Uberti, Baschiera di messer Bindo della Tosa, Baldinaccio Adimari, Giovanni de' Cerchi, Naldo di messer Lottino Gherardini, and several others. And the names of those representing the Black Party, who were in Florence, were messer Corso Donati, messer Rosso della Tosa, messer Pazzino de' Pazzi, messer Geri Spini, messer Maruccio Cavalcanti, messer Berto Brunelleschi, and several others.

When these members of the White Party entered Florence, they were greatly honored by the common people. Many old Ghibelline men and women kissed the Uberti arms; and Lapo di messer Azzolino was closely guarded by their magnate friends, since members of his house bore the mortal hatred of many Guelf citizens.[17]

Baschiera della Tosa was also greatly honored, and he honored messer Rosso in word and deed. The *popolo* took great hope from this, because the Whites and Ghibellines planned to let themselves be led by the Blacks and agree to whatever was demanded of them, so that the Blacks would have no excuse to avoid peace. But the Blacks had no desire for peace. They strung the others along with so many words that the Whites were advised to gather at the Cavalcanti house and there fortify themselves with friends and not leave their city. Many wise men said that if the Whites had done this, they would have been victorious. But they sent messengers to the Cavalcanti, on

16. Other sources say instead that there were twelve representatives, one Ghibelline and one White Guelf from each sixth of the city.

17. This was the first time since 1258 that any member of the Uberti family had set foot in Florence.

their own behalf and that of the cardinal, to request their permission. The Cavalcanti took counsel and decided not to receive them. This was widely considered to be a bad decision for them, for they and their houses suffered great harm from fire and other things, as I will recount later.

After the Whites had been turned away by the Cavalcanti, and when they noted the suspicious appearance of their foes and the words they used, they were advised to leave; and they did so on June 8, 1304. The cardinal remained. Those who did not look kindly on him acted as if they might harm him; and one family named the Quaratesi, neighbors of the Mozzi and of the palace where the cardinal was staying, pretended to shoot at him. When he complained about this, he was advised to leave. He departed in fear on June 9, leaving the city in a bad state, and went off to Perugia where the pope was.

8   The good citizens were left very troubled and despaired of peace. The Cavalcanti and many others complained, and spirits grew so heated that people took arms and began to harm one another. The della Tosa and Medici came into the Old Market armed with crossbows, shooting towards the Corso degli Adimari and down through Via Calimala. They attacked and destroyed a barricade in the Corso, which was guarded by people who were more eager for vengeance than for peace.

Messer Rossellino della Tosa with his brigade went to set the Sassetti house on fire.[18] The Cavalcanti and other people came to its rescue. In that crush Nerone Cavalcanti came against messer Rossellino; he leveled his lance and struck messer Rossellino on the chest, knocking him off his horse.

The leaders of the Black Party, thinking that it was time to start a brawl, had prepared a Greek fire. They had come to an agreement with a certain ser Neri Abati, prior of San Piero Scheraggio, a wicked and dissolute man and an enemy of his kinsmen, and arranged that he set the first fire. And so he set it on June 10, 1304, in the house of his kinsmen in Piazza Or San Michele. Fire also was shot from the Old Market into Via Calimala; and since no one fought it, it spread until it joined with the first and burned many houses, palaces, and shops.

There was a large loggia in Piazza Or San Michele with an oratory of Our Lady which contained many wax devotional images. They caught fire, adding to the heat of the air, and burned all the houses around that place, the warehouses in Via Calimala, all the shops around the Old Market all the way

18. The Sassetti were Ghibellines.

to the New Market and the Cavalcanti houses, and Via Vacchereccia and Via Porta Santa Maria all the way to the Ponte Vecchio. It was said that more than nineteen hundred houses burned; and nothing could be done to stop the fire.

Thieves brazenly went into the fire to steal and carry off whatever they could grab, and nothing was said to them. Even someone who saw his own goods being carried off did not dare ask for them, because the city was in bad shape in every way.

That day the Cavalcanti lost their heart and nerve as they watched their houses and palaces and shops burn, for the high rents in that crowded place had kept them rich.

Many citizens, afraid of the fire, cleared their belongings off to some other place which they believed would be safe from the fire. But it spread so far that many lost out for trying to escape it and were left ruined.

The truth about this misdeed—why the fire was set, and set in that place—should be known. It was the leaders of the Black Party who prepared this fire in Ognissanti in order to flush out the Cavalcanti, whom they feared because of their wealth and power. This fire was composed in such a way that when some of it fell on the ground it left a blue color. Ser Neri Abati carried this fire in a pot and set it in his kinsmen's house, and messer Rosso della Tosa and others shot it into Via Calimala.

Sinibaldo di messer Corso Donati carried a big batch of this fire, like a lit torch, to set fire to the Cavalcanti houses in the New Market; and Boccaccio Adimari with his followers came through Corso degli Adimari up to Or San Michele. The Cavalcanti went to meet them, and pushed them back in the Corso and captured a barricade they had made. Then the Blacks set fire to the Macci house in Corte delle Badesse.

The podestà of the city went to the New Market with his followers and many soldiers, but he gave no help or protection. They stayed on their horses and watched the fire and got in the way because of the encumbrance they made, obstructing the footsoldiers and passersby.

The Cavalcanti and many others watched the fire and did not have the courage to go against their enemies after the fire was spent, though they could have won and remained lords. Messer Maruccio Cavalcanti and messer Rinieri Lucardesi urged them to take lit torches and go burn the houses of the foes who had burned theirs. But they did not follow this advice, though if they had they would have been victorious, since the other faction prepared no defense. Sad and mournful, they went to their kinsmen's houses; and their enemies grew bold and chased them from the city. They went to their estates, this one to Ostina and that one to the Stinche; and many went to Siena because the Sienese held out the hope of reconciliation. And so time passed and no reconciliation came, and everyone considered the Cavalcanti cowards.

9   The citizens of Florence were left bewildered and dismayed by this dangerous fire, and they did not dare to complain because those who had set it held the government tyrannically. Besides, even the rulers had lost many of their belongings.

The leaders of the ruling group, knowing that they would surely be denounced to the Holy Father, decided to go to the Papal Court in Perugia. Those who went were messer Corso Donati, messer Rosso della Tosa, messer Pazzino de' Pazzi, messer Geri Spini, and messer Betto Brunelleschi, with several Lucchese and Sienese. They believed that with artful words and money and the backing of friends they could nullify their offense against the cardinal, legate and peacemaker in Tuscany, and the great infamy of the fire they had most cruelly set in the city. They arrived at the Papal Court, where they began to sow the seeds they brought.

On July 22, 1304, Pope Benedict XI died in Perugia of poison, which had been put in some fresh figs he was given.[19]

10   While these men were staying in Perugia, the Florentine exiles had a bold idea: that they should secretly summon all those who were of their mind to gather fully armed at a specified place and time. They managed the arrangements so secretly that those who had stayed in Florence heard nothing. They put themselves in order and arrived suddenly at Lastra, only two miles from Florence, with twelve hundred men at arms on horseback wearing white surcoats; and the Bolognese, Romagnoles, Aretines, and other friends were there, on horse and foot.

A great outcry spread through the city. The Blacks were terrified of their foes and began to speak humble words. Many hid themselves in monasteries and many disguised themselves as friars out of fear of their enemies, for they were unprepared and had no other refuge.

When the Whites and Ghibellines were at Lastra, many of their friends within the city went one night to urge them to come quickly. This was in July, the day of St. Mary Magdalen on the 21st, and it was very hot.[20] And

19. Giovanni Villani also says that the pope was poisoned, though he gives the date as July 27. However, a source closer to the event (the *Brevi Annali di Perugia dal 1194 al 1352*) says that Benedict XI died on July 7 of natural causes.

20. Most other sources give the date as July 20, the feast day of St. Margaret.

all the people who were supposed to assemble had not yet arrived, because the first to come showed themselves two days early.

Messer Tolosato degli Uberti and the Pistoiese had not yet arrived, since it was not the appointed day. The Cavalcanti, the Gherardini, the Lucardesi, and the Scolari had not yet come down from the Val di Pesa. But Baschiera, who was more or less the captain, was won over more by desire than by reason, just like a youth. Finding himself with a good troop and under strong pressure to act, he thought that he could win the prestige of victory and so swooped down on the city with his knights, so that they were in open view. And they should not have done this, for night was a better friend to them than daytime—because of the day's heat, and because their friends would have gone to them by night from the city, and because they broke the terms of the agreement with their friends. Their friends did not reveal themselves because it was not the prearranged hour.

They approached San Gallo and drew themselves up in the bishop's farmstead near San Marco, with white banners unfurled and olive garlands and bared swords, crying "peace," without doing violence or despoiling anyone. They were a fine sight, standing in formation with the olive branches of peace. The heat was so great that the air seemed to burn. Their skirmishers on foot and horse drew close to the city and came to the Porta degli Spadai, believing that Baschiera's friends would be there and that they could enter without opposition. And so they did not advance in order, with axes and weapons to force open the gate. The barricades of San Gallo were defended against them, but they broke them and wounded many Gangalandesi who were on guard there. They reached the gate, and many of them entered the city through the postern. But the people in the city who had made them promises did not keep their pacts. These included the Pazzi, the Magalotti, and messer Lambertuccio Frescobaldi, who were angry with their own Black Party because of the outrages and insults they had suffered and the fire set in the city and other villainies done to them. Instead, these people went against the Whites to show that they were not traitors; they strove to outdo the rest in harming the Whites, and came towards Santa Reparata shooting with crank-loading crossbows.[21]

But nothing would have been of any avail if a fire had not been set in a palace next to the city gate. Those who had already entered the city feared they were betrayed and turned back. They carried off the postern gate and rejoined the main body, which had not budged. And the fire grew rapidly.

---

21. These bows, which were bent by means of a crank, were more powerful than ordinary crossbows.

In this situation, Baschiera realized that those who should have supported him were opposing him, and therefore he wheeled the horses and turned back. And the Whites' hope and joy changed to mourning, for their conquered enemies became conquerors and took heart like lions. They raced in pursuit, but very carefully. The footsoldiers, overcome by the sun's heat, flung themselves among the vineyards and houses seeking shelter, and many collapsed from heat and exhaustion.

Baschiera dashed into the monastery of San Domenico and took away by force two very rich nephews of his, whom he led off with him. And God punished him for this.

Many noblemen stopped at Carlettino de' Pazzi's house to gather their forces and harm the foes they were pursuing. And they did not follow them any more.

A short distance from the city they [22] encountered messer Tolosato degli Uberti, who was coming with the Pistoiese to be there on the appointed day. He wanted to turn them around, but could not. He returned to Pistoia with great sorrow because of this, and he was well aware that Baschiera's childishness had cost him the city.

The Blacks killed many exiles whom they found hiding and many poor invalids whom they dragged out of hospitals. They captured many Bolognese and Aretines, and hanged them all. And the following day those who were cunning spread a false rumor that messer Corso Donati and messer Cante de' Gabrielli da Gubbio had taken Arezzo by treason. Their enemies were so frightened by this that they lost their vigor and did not dare to move.

11 And so, thanks to a great mistake, the Whites lost the city they had nearly regained. And many said that they would have taken the city if they had come by any other gate, for there were no defenders except for a few youths who would not have put themselves so far forward as to risk dying. Gherarduccio di messer Buondelmonte did just that: he pursued the Whites so closely that one of them turned back and awaited him, and leveled his lance and struck him to the ground.

The exiles' plan had been wise and vigorous; but its execution was mad because they were too hasty and came before the prearranged day. The Aretines and Bolognese carried off the postern gate, to the great shame of the Blacks.

Events are often the test of men, who are great not because of virtue, but

22. The retreating exiles.

simply by reputation. And this was seen on that day when the Whites came to the city, for many citizens changed their speech, dress, and manners. Even those who used to speak most proudly against the exiles changed their tune and proclaimed in the piazzas and other places how fine it was that the exiles would return home. And it was fear rather than reason or their wishes that made them say this. Many took refuge among the religious orders, not out of humility but out of vile and miserable cowardice, believing that the city was lost. But once the Whites had left, they began once again to use their former wicked, provocative, and mendacious words.

12 Divine justice, which often punishes in hidden ways, and takes good pastors away from wicked people who do not deserve them and gives them instead that which their malice deserves, took from them Pope Benedict. In June, 1305, through the will of the king of France and the efforts of the Colonna, the cardinals elected pope messer Ramondo de Got, archbishop of Bordeaux in Gascony, who took the name Clement V.[23] He did not leave that side of the Alps and come to Rome, but was consecrated at Lyons on the Rhone. It was said that at his consecration the place collapsed in ruins, and that the crown fell from his head, and that the king of France would not let him leave there.[24] At the king's request he created many cardinals from that side of the Alps and arranged many tithes and other things; but when asked to publicly declare Pope Boniface a heretic, he would never do so.[25]

13 Cardinal Niccolò of Prato, who had strongly supported his election, was very much in his good graces. And when he was legate in Tuscany (as was said earlier), he had been given authority by the Pistoiese to appoint their officials for four years, so that he would have the authority to dispose of Pistoia in whatever way the peace agreement might stipulate. For the Black Party wanted their Guelf exiles to return to Pistoia, saying: "We will not make peace if Pistoia does not put itself in order; for if we are pacified, the Ghibellines will still hold Pistoia since messer Tolosato is its lord. And so

---

23. An error for Bertrand de Got.

24. During the coronation ceremonies at Lyons on November 11, 1305, a wall collapsed under the weight of the spectators. This occurred just as the pope passed in front of the wall, seated upon a horse led by the king of France and Charles of Valois. A cardinal and a brother of the pope were killed; the pope himself fell off the horse. This was taken to be a sign of God's wrath at the abandonment of the traditional seat of the papacy.

25. Clement V did nearly everything the king of France asked him to do. However, he refused to condemn Boniface as a heretic, exhume and burn his corpse, and scatter the ashes.

we would be tricked." And Pistoia was said to belong to the Church. But the cardinal's promise was not effective, because he was chased from Florence, as I said.

When the Blacks had lost all hope of being given Pistoia, they decided to take it by force. They went there and laid siege to it with the help of the Lucchese. They fortified themselves and barricaded the city and built thick siege towers with many guards.

The city was tiny and set in the plain; but it was strongly walled and crenellated, with fortresses and war-gates and great moats of water so that it could not be taken by storm. And so the Blacks tried to starve Pistoia, since it could expect no relief. Their friends the Pisans helped the Pistoiese with money, but not with men; the Bolognese were no great friends of the Pistoiese.

14 The Blacks chose for their war captain Duke Robert of Calabria, eldest son of King Charles of Apulia, who came to Florence with three hundred horsemen.[26] They and the Lucchese stayed a long time at the siege, because the Pistoiese—men of great personal valor—often sallied out to come to blows with their enemies and performed deeds of great prowess. They killed many men from the countryside of Florence and Lucca, and defended their city with few people because want had constrained many to leave it. Because they had not expected to be besieged, they had not provided themselves with supplies; and once they were besieged, they could not.

And so they were afflicted by hunger. The officials in charge of provisions wisely hid them in various places. At night the women and men unfit to fight slipped through the camp, and went to Sambuca and other places and towns in the direction of Bologna for supplies, and easily brought them to Pistoia. The Florentines, hearing of this, fortified that side so that little could be brought in. Still, with money and stealth the Pistoiese got some food in, until the ditch was completed and siege towers built. From then on nothing could be brought in, since whoever carried it was captured and his nose or feet cut off. And this so dismayed them that no one dared to bring in any more provisions.

The lords and governors of Pistoia did not want to abandon their city, for they were men who hoped to defend themselves. The Pisans helped them with money, but not with men. Because of the shortage of food, messer

26. Robert of Calabria was the third son of Charles II of Anjou, but his two older brothers had died.

Tolosato degli Uberti and Agnolo di messer Guiglielmino [de' Pazzi], the magistrates, sent away all of the poor, the children, the widows, and almost all the other women of low status.

Oh what a cruel thing this was for the citizens' spirits to bear: to watch as their women were led to the city gates, placed in the hands of their enemies, and locked outside. And those who did not have powerful relatives outside, or who were not received out of gentility, were raped by their enemies. The Pistoiese exiles, recognizing the women and children of their foes, raped a number of them; but Duke Robert protected many.

At the petition of cardinal Niccolò of Prato, the new pope Clement V ordered Duke Robert and the Florentines to raise the siege of Pistoia. The duke obeyed and left; the Florentines remained there, and chose as captain messer [Bino] de' Gabrielli da Gubbio, who had no pity for the citizens of Pistoia.[27] Those inside the city held back their tears and did not show their anguish, for they saw that it was necessary to do this to avoid dying. They vented their feelings on their enemies: when they captured anyone, they killed him cruelly. But the great pity was those who had been mutilated in the camp, who were set at the foot of the walls with their feet cut off so their fathers, brothers, or sons could see them. And the Pistoiese could not take in the victims or help them because their rulers would not allow it, to keep the others from becoming dismayed; nor did the rulers let relatives and friends of the victims watch from the wall. And so the good Pistoiese citizens died, mutilated by their enemies and driven towards their troubled and afflicted city.

Sodom and Gomorrah and other cities which were suddenly swallowed and their inhabitants killed met a much better fate than the Pistoiese, who died in such bitter torments. Oh how the wrath of God assailed them! How many sins had they committed, and of what sort, to merit such a violent judgment? Even the besiegers outside the city suffered many troubles because of the bad weather and poor terrain and great costs. The besiegers taxed their own citizens heavily and despoiled the Whites and Ghibellines of their money, so that they consumed many fortunes.

They devised a very clever way of raising money: a levy known as the Saw which they placed on the citizens. They assessed the Ghibellines and Whites so much per head per day—three *lire* for some, two or one *lira* for others, according to how much they thought each could bear. Those who

27. Duke Robert of Calabria left the siege in October, but his troops remained behind. The new captain, Bino, was the brother of Cante de' Gabrielli, the podestà who had condemned the leaders of the White Guelfs (see above, II, 19 and 25).

were banished had to pay imposts just like those who lived in the city. And they laid a special impost on all fathers who had sons able to bear arms, if the son did not go to serve in the army within twenty days. They sent the men of each sixth [of Florence] in turn, in shifts of twenty days. And the Florentines and Lucchese managed to ruin many of their peasants by making them serve without pay, for they were poor men who had to stay in arms at the siege of Pistoia.

The governors of Pistoia, who knew where the provisions were hidden, always kept them concealed. They carefully doled them out to the foreigners who served the city in arms and to the other useful men as they were needed, because they saw death from starvation drawing near.

Those who knew how short supplies were faced hard choices. Their plan was to maintain themselves as long as possible, and then tell the people. At that time they would all take arms and like desperate men fling themselves on their enemies with swords in hand. "Either we will die with nothing to lose, or perhaps our enemies will lose heart and hide and throw themselves into flight or other cowardly expedients." They planned to do this when they saw themselves come to the end of their supplies. And nevertheless they did not abandon all hope of escaping.

15   The Pistoiese informed the cardinal from Prato of their miserable straits, and also their other secret friends on the outside who were working on their behalf. And as a result of their efforts at the Papal Court messer Napoleone Orsini was named cardinal legate in Tuscany and in the Patriarchate of Aquileia. This was done to succor Pistoia, as a city subject to the Church. The cardinal set out at once, and in a few days he arrived in Lombardy.

Our glorious God, who afflicts and chastises sinners but does not confound them utterly, was moved to pity. He planted in the minds of the Florentines this thought: "This cardinal is coming, and when he arrives he will say that Pistoia belongs to the Church. He will want to enter it, and so we will fall out with the Church." And they set their minds to devising some solution.

Things are feared more from afar than when they are close at hand, since man imagines many things—as when a fortress or castle is being built there are many who fear it for various reasons, yet once it is built and finished their minds are reassured and they do not fear it at all. Just so the Florentines feared the cardinal from afar, and up close paid him little heed. And yet there were reasons to fear him: because of the majesty of the Church, because of his office, because of his great status in Rome, and because of his great friendship with lords and communes.[28] And the Florentines feared his arrival so much that they decided to seek an accord in the following fashion.

There was a wise and good friar of Santo Spirito whom they sent to Pistoia to see his good friend messer [Filippo] de' Vergellesi, one of the leading citizens of that city.[29] In speaking with him, the friar made many specific and general promises on behalf of the government of Florence, offering to leave the city free and its buildings intact, and the persons and their castles safe.

When the knight [messer Filippo] heard this offer, he told the Elders about it. They considered what the friar said and the authority he held, and concluded the agreement—not without the will of God, who disposes of things great and small, and did not want to undo that city completely. O pious mercy, how you brought them to the brink of extremity! For they only had enough provisions to live for a single day, and then the citizens had to be told they faced death from starvation. May you, most holy Majesty, be forever praised for this, for pigs would have rejected the bread those good citizens were eating.

The accord was reached before the cardinal's arrival, and the gates were opened on April 10, 1306. And there were some citizens who, because of the hunger they had suffered, ate so much that they burst.

The Blacks of Florence occupied Pistoia and did not keep their agreements. They were so oppressed by fear that they might have to give up the city that immediately and without the slightest pause they tore down the walls, which were so beautiful.

The cardinal legate was very annoyed when he heard the news from Pistoia, for he believed that he would have been able to find some remedy. He went off to Bologna and there established his residence.

16 Parma, Reggio, and Bologna rebelled against the marquis of Ferrara.[30] Because of the overweening tyranny with which the marquis ruled those cities, God did not wish to support him any longer; and when he was at the height of his power, he fell. For he had taken as wife the daughter of King Charles of Apulia; and so that King Charles would consent to give her

28. The Orsini, like the Colonna, were one of the great families of Rome.

29. Compagni could not recall the given name of this knight.

30. Compagni here begins to widen the scope of his chronicle, as other cities become involved in the struggle between the Black Guelfs and the exiles. But since he had less opportunity to gather detailed information about these more distant events, his account of them is less precise. In this case, for instance, Parma was not ruled by the marquis of Ferrara, but by Giberto da Correggio. It was Giberto who incited Modena and Reggio to rebel, as Compagni notes at the end of this paragraph.

to him, he bought her—in violation of common practice—by giving her Modena and Reggio in dowry.[31] His brothers and the noble citizens disdained to acknowledge fealty to someone else; and to this disdain was added the enmity of a powerful knight of Parma named messer Giberto, whom the marquis had treacherously sought to drive out. This knight strongly incited the citizens of Modena and Reggio to rebel, and with men and arms he freed them from servitude.

17　While the legate was in Bologna, the Bolognese rebelled and drove out their enemies.[32] The legate thought that he could pacify them. The Florentines employed their money and suggestions so effectively that they fixed on him the blame for a plot to betray Bologna. He was expelled from Bologna vilely and shamefully, and one of his chaplains was killed there.[33] He went to Forlì in the Romagna, but the Florentines denied him entrance. He went to Arezzo and from there sought to humble the Florentines with letters and embassies, but without success.

The cardinal gathered many soldiers and made himself strong in Arezzo, where he was staying, for he understood that the Blacks of Florence would go against him in force. The marquis of the March of Ancona came to his aid, along with many nobles from that area, White Guelfs and Ghibellines from Florence, and mounted men from Rome and Pisa in the service of many Lombard clerics. It was estimated that a total of twenty-four hundred picked horsemen assembled there.

The Blacks of Florence set out, but very cautiously. They did not approach Arezzo: instead they took the route towards Siena, then turned through the mountains and entered Aretine territory, where they destroyed many of the Ubertini strongholds. The Blacks did not descend to the plain since the passes could have been held against them; and they did not give battle since they feared the outcome. Their enemies urged the cardinal to give battle, arguing that he held a great advantage and victory was sure. But the cardinal would not agree to attack, nor occupy the passes nor seize the Blacks' provisions as they left. And so the Blacks returned to Florence without any trouble or damage.

31. In April of 1305, Azzo VIII of Ferrara married Beatrice of Anjou, daughter of Charles II. It was said at the time that Azzo gave Charles more than twenty thousand florins and assigned Modena and Reggio to Beatrice. This was the reverse of the usual practice, by which a dowry given by the father of the bride went with her on her marriage.

32. Cardinal Orsini was in Bologna late in April, after the fall of Pistoia.

33. He was expelled from Bologna on May 22, 1306.

The cardinal was harshly criticized for having let the Blacks get away safely. Many people said that he had done it for money, or because of a promise the Blacks had made to obey and honor him. Or rather, that messer Corso Donati had promised the cardinal four thousand florins in exchange for the city; and the cardinal went towards Florence with his men in order to draw the Blacks' army from Aretine territory, and so get the money but not give messer Corso the city.

The people who had come in support of the cardinal left disconsolate, because they saw the game was up. They had spent a lot of money, thinking they could win back their city, but without any result. And they never assembled again.

18 The Blacks mocked the cardinal and sought to heap scorn on him in many ways, while acting as if they wished to obey him. After they returned to Florence, they sent him as ambassadors messer Betto Brunelleschi and messer Geri Spini, who made him turn and spin to their tune, extracting favors from him and acting like the lords of his court. And so they had him send a certain friar Ubertino to the *signori*; and they found so many reasons and put forward so many excuses from one moment to the next that the exiles awaited the new *signori*, hoping that they would be more favorable.

Some said that the cardinal thought that the Blacks were just men, and he confidently told his friends that there would be peace. Never was a woman charmed and then abused by ruffians the way this man was by those two knights. And it was said that the younger one did his job more subtly, leading the cardinal with words and pursuing peace negotiations; his sort of talk kept them busy a good long time.

Finally, because of the bad report about the cardinal that reached the Papal Court, he was removed from his legation; and he went to Rome with little honor.

The wise men realized that these ambassadors were in Arezzo to stir up discord among the Aretines. And Uguccione della Faggiuola, together with the Magalotti and many nobles, sowed such discord in Arezzo that the powerful Ghibellines were at each other's throats; but then they settled down.[34]

19 Just as a worm is born in a solid apple, so all things created for a certain purpose must carry within themselves the cause which brings them

---

34. The Ghibelline party, which ruled Arezzo, was split (like the Guelfs of Florence) into two factions. Uguccione was the head of one of these factions; the turmoil followed his return to Arezzo in 1308, and ended with his assumption of power.

to that end. Among the Black Guelfs of Florence, great discord sprang once again from envy and greed. It seemed to messer Corso Donati that he had worked hardest to regain the city but won little or no part of the offices and profits, whereas messer Rosso della Tosa, messer Pazzino de' Pazzi, messer Betto Brunelleschi, and messer Geri Spini, with their followers among the *popolo*, took the offices, served their friends, made the decisions, and did the favors—and brought him low. And so their dislike for one another began to increase, and it grew so much that it came to open hatred.

One day messer Pazzino de' Pazzi had messer Corso Donati arrested because of some money that messer Corso owed him. They exchanged many rude words, because the others wanted to rule without messer Corso. They feared his proud spirit and energy, and did not believe that he could be satisfied with a share of power.

So messer Corso gathered many sorts of people to his side. He had a large part of the magnates, since they hated the strong Ordinances of Justice which the *popolani* had passed against them and which he promised to annul.[35] He attracted many with hopes of becoming so great with him that they would remain in power, and others with fine words, which he colored well. Throughout the city he said: "These men appropriate all the offices and the rest of us, although we are noble and powerful men, are treated like strangers. These men have bodyguards who follow them around. These men have the false *popolani*, and they share out the treasure which we, as leading citizens, should control."[36] And so he persuaded many of his adversaries and brought them to his point of view. Among them were the Medici and the Bordoni, who used to be his enemies and supporters of messer Rosso della Tosa.

When messer Corso had rebuilt his faction, they began to speak more arrogantly in the piazzas and in the councils; and if someone opposed them, they treated him like an enemy. And the fire grew so hot that, by agreement of this faction, the Medici and the Bordoni and others delegated to the job attacked Scambrilla to kill him, but only wounded him several times in the face. Their adversaries held that this was done to spite them; they visited Scambrilla often and had a lot to say, and when he was healed they provided him with guards at public expense and urged him to make a great vendetta.

35. The Ordinances of Justice had been reinforced on December 23, 1306; Compagni's concern with events in northern Italy led him to omit mention of this important domestic development.

36. By "false *popolani*" Corso meant the *popolani grassi*, rich citizens who were *popolani* only in name.

This Scambrilla was strong physically and strong in the friendship of those he served; but he was not a man of high status, for he had been a hired soldier.

With hatred growing because of the arrogant words exchanged by the men of messer Corso's faction and the others, they all began to bring in men and friends from every side. The Bordoni had a great following from Carmignano, Pistoia, and Monte di Sotto, as well as from Taio di messer Rodolfo, a great man of Prato, and the men of his household and his opinion, who gave great assistance to the conspirators.

Messer Corso had greatly aroused the Lucchese, pointing out the wicked deeds of his adversaries and the means they employed; whether what he said was true or false, he knew how to color it well. Back in Florence, he arranged that on a specified day they should all take arms and go to the palace of the *signori*, and say that they absolutely wanted Florence to have a different government; and upon these words, come to blows.

20 Messer Rosso and his followers heard of these gatherings, the words that were being said, and the preparation of arms. Their irate spirits became so inflamed with talk that they could not hold back from havoc. One Sunday morning they went to the *signori*, who called the Council and took arms.[37] They summoned messer Corso, his sons, and the Bordoni; but the summons and the sentence were issued in the same breath and they were instantly condemned. On that same day the *popolo* went in furor to messer Corso's house. He barricaded himself in Piazza San Piero Maggiore and reinforced himself with many troops; the Bordoni hurried there vigorously with a large following and with pennants showing their arms.

Messer Corso was badly afflicted with gout and could not bear arms, but he urged his friends on with his tongue, praising and inspiring those who bore themselves valiantly. But he had few men, for it was not the day he had chosen.

The attackers were numerous, for all the banners of the *popolo* were there alongside the mercenaries and men at arms, attacking the barricades with crossbows, stones, and fire. Messer Corso's few soldiers defended themselves vigorously with lances, crossbows, and stones, waiting for those in the conspiracy to come to their aid—that is, the Bardi, the Rossi, the Frescobaldi, almost all of the sixth of Oltrarno, the Tornaquinci, and the Buondelmonti, except for messer Gherardo. But none of them showed any sign of coming.

37. October 6, 1308.

Seeing that he could no longer defend himself, messer Corso decided to leave. The barricades were broken; his friends fled through the houses. And many of his partisans pretended to belong to the other party.

Messer Rosso, messer Pazzino, messer Geri, Pinaccio, and many others fought vigorously on foot and horse. Piero and messer Guiglielmino Spini (a fresh young knight armed in Catalan style), together with Boccaccio Adimari and his sons and some of his relatives, pursued Gherardo Bordoni closely and caught him at Croce a Gorgo. They attacked him; he fell headlong. They dismounted and killed him, and Boccaccio's son cut off his hand and carried it home. Some people condemned him for this. He said he did it because Gherardo had opposed them at the request of messer Tedice Adimari, their kinsman and Gherardo's brother-in-law. Gherardo's brothers escaped, and his father took refuge in the Tornaquinci house, for he was old.

21 Messer Corso, ill with gout, fled towards the abbey of San Salvi, since he had already commanded and performed many evil deeds. The men at arms caught him and recognized him, and wanted to lead him off; he defended himself with fine words like a wise knight. Meanwhile, the marshal's young brother-in-law arrived. Though urged by the others to kill messer Corso, he refused to do it and turned back. He was sent again, and this second time he struck messer Corso in the throat with a Catalan lance and another blow in the flank, and knocked him to the ground. Some monks carried messer Corso to the abbey, and there he died on September [. . .], 1307, and was buried.[38]

The people began to settle down. Messer Corso's bad death was talked about in various ways, according to whether the speaker was his friend or enemy. But to tell the truth, he lived dangerously and died reprehensibly. He was a knight of great spirit and renown, noble in blood and behavior, and very handsome in appearance even in his old age, of fine form with delicate features and white skin. He was a charming, wise, and elegant speaker, and always undertook great things. He was accustomed to dealing familiarly with great lords and noble men, and had many friends, and was famous throughout all Italy. He was the enemy of the *popolo* and of *popolani*, and was loved by his soldiers; he was full of malicious thoughts, cruel and astute. He was killed in this vile manner by a foreign mercenary; and messer Corso's relatives knew full well who killed him, for the killer was imme-

---

38. Dino Compagni was unsure of the exact date; Corso Donati actually died on October 6, 1308.

diately sent away by his companions. Everyone commonly said that the ones who ordered his death were messer Rosso della Tosa and messer Pazzino de' Pazzi; and some people blessed them, while others did the opposite. Many believed that these two knights had him killed. And I, wishing to discover the truth, inquired diligently and found this to be true.[39]

22　The holy Church of Rome, which is mother to Christians when wicked pastors do not lead it astray, had fallen into low esteem as the reverence of the faithful diminished. It summoned the Florentines, held a trial of excommunication, and pronounced sentence against them; it excommunicated the officials, interdicted the city, and deprived laymen of the holy mass.[40] The Florentines sent ambassadors to the pope.[41] Bishop Lottieri della Tosa died, and a new bishop was named through simony: a man of low birth, zealous for the Guelf Party and beloved by the *popolo*, but not of holy life.[42]

The pope was widely condemned for this, though wrongly: according to the philosopher, evil pastors are sometimes sent by God because of the sins of the people. Many people lavished promises and money on the Papal Court: some had the votes and others had the money, but this man got the bishopric. One of the cathedral canons was elected bishop by the canons. Messer Rosso and the others favored him, because he was of their mind and they thought they could bend him as they wished. He went to the Papal Court and spent a lot of money, but did not get the bishopric.

23　The imperial throne was left vacant after the death of Frederick II.[43] Those who supported the imperial party were oppressed by heavy burdens and had almost vanished from Tuscany and Sicily. Governments had changed, and the fame of the Empire had nearly vanished from human memory. But then the Emperor of heaven took matters in hand and planted in the minds of the pope and his cardinals an awareness that the strength of the holy Church had grown so feeble that the faithful hardly obeyed it.

39. But see below, III, 39, where Dino says that it was Betto Brunelleschi who was largely responsible for Corso's death.

40. Compagni here alludes to a whole series of interdicts and excommunications issued against Florence, and especially the most recent one, pronounced by Cardinal Orsini in 1307 when he resigned his office of peacemaker.

41. Envoys were sent in 1309, and in September they were granted a bull of absolution.

42. He was Antonio d'Orso, who had been bishop of Fiesole.

43. Since the death of Frederick II in 1250, no king of Germany had assumed the title of Holy Roman Emperor.

The king of France swelled with pride because he had brought about the death of Pope Boniface. He believed that his strength kept everyone cowed. He frightened the pope into naming cardinals to his liking, demanded that the bones of Pope Boniface be burned and he be sentenced as a heretic, detained the pope almost by force, oppressed and persecuted the Jews to despoil them of their money, threatened the Templars and charged them with heresy, and debased the honor of the holy Church. Because of all these novelties, the Church was no longer respected in men's minds. Since it had neither strength nor protector, the pope and cardinals thought of creating an emperor, a man who was just, wise, and powerful, a son of Holy Church and a lover of the faith. They searched assiduously for someone who would be worthy of such an honor. And they found a man who had resided at length at the Papal Court, a wise man of noble blood, just and renowned, very loyal, bold in arms and noble in lineage, a man of great intelligence and great temperance—that is, Henry, count of Luxembourg in the Rhine valley of Germany, forty years of age, of medium height, a good speaker and fine looking, although slightly cross-eyed.

This count had been at the Papal Court to obtain a great archbishopric in Germany for his brother, and he left after obtaining this benefice. This archbishop was one of the seven electors of the emperor. By God's will, the other electors agreed and Henry was elected emperor; and after the long vacancy of the Empire, he thought being king meant almost nothing.

24 Cardinal Niccolò of Prato had strongly supported Henry's election, expecting that the emperor would help his friends and punish his enemies and adversaries; he abandoned every other hope as insignificant and relied on the majesty of this man. Henry was elected emperor on July 16, 1309,[44] and he was confirmed and the letters sealed in the same year. After being elected and confirmed, he crossed the Alps, for he had promised and sworn to come receive the crown the following August and he was a faithful lord who intended to keep his oath. In his first council Henry was offended by the Florentines, because at their instance the archbishop of Mainz advised him not to go and said that it was enough for him to be king of Germany, whereas the trip to Italy seemed very uncertain and dangerous.

Omnipotent God, the guardian and guide of princes, wanted Henry to come strike down and punish the tyrants of Lombardy and Tuscany, until all

---

44. An error: Henry received papal confirmation on July 26, 1309; he had been elected emperor in 1308.

tyranny was extinguished.⁴⁵ The emperor fixed his mind on keeping his promise, like a lord who respected his faith. Henry crossed the Alps through the lands of the count of Savoy, with few knights and without arms since that area was safe, and he arrived at Asti at the promised time. There he gathered men and took arms and exhorted his knights. He came down until he was near Milan, passing from city to city, making peace as if he were an angel of God and receiving fealty. And he was strongly opposed by King Robert, who was in Lombardy.⁴⁶

2 5   The emperor arrived at the intersection of two roads, one of which led to Milan and the other to Pavia. A noble knight named messer Matteo Visconti raised his hand and said: "Lord, this hand can give and take Milan for you. Come to Milan, where my friends are, so that no one will be able to take it from us. If you go towards Pavia, you will lose Milan." Messer Matteo had been a rebel against Milan for many years and was captain of nearly all of Lombardy; he was a man more wise and astute than loyal. The captain and lord of Milan at that time was messer Guidotto della Torre, a loyal lord but not so wise. The della Torre were noblemen of ancient lineage; their arms consisted of a tower in the middle of the right side of the shield, and on the other side two lilies crossed. And they were enemies of the Visconti.

The emperor sent to Milan one of his marshals, a della Torre by birth, who spoke many friendly words to messer Guidotto and displayed Henry's good will.⁴⁷ But messer Guidotto still distrusted Henry's arrival and feared he would lose his lordship, though he was not willing to undertake war in his defense. He had all his soldiers wear the [Guelf] Party markings—a white field with a vermilion band—and he had many bridges destroyed for some distance from the city. The emperor, unperturbed, took the advice of messer Matteo Visconti and headed towards Milan, passing by Pavia on the right hand.

Count Filippone, the lord of Pavia, appeared ready to honor Henry in

45. Henry's expedition to Italy stirred the hopes of the Ghibellines and the Whites, including Dante and Dino Compagni. The story of Henry's expedition forms the concluding portion of the chronicle, which reaches its climax with Henry's coronation in Rome.

46. In May 1309 Duke Robert of Calabria had succeeded his father, Charles II of Anjou, as king of Apulia. At this time he was in northern Italy, lending his aid to the Guelf Party there.

47. The marshal sent to Milan was in fact Henry of Flanders. However, there were in the imperial camp two della Torre, exiled from Milan by their uncle Guidotto; perhaps one of them accompanied the marshal.

Pavia with great good will.[48] The emperor, following the direct route towards Milan, crossed the Tesino at a ford and rode through the district without opposition.

The Milanese went forth to meet Henry. When messer Guidotto saw all the *popolo* going to meet the emperor, he went too. And when he came before Henry, messer Guidotto threw his scepter to the earth, dismounted on the ground, and kissed his feet. Like a man bewitched, he did the opposite of what he wished to do.

26 The emperor was welcomed to Milan by the *popolo* with great pomp. He made peace between messer Guidotto and messer Matteo, together with their followers; and he did many other fine things and held many assemblies. He sent many letters to Germany, having heard that his son had been crowned king of Bohemia and had taken a new wife, which gave him great joy.[49]

It was the ancient custom for the emperor to receive the first crown at Monza.[50] But to show his love for the Milanese and to avoid turning back, he and his wife received the iron crown in Milan, in the church of Sant'Ambrogio on the morning of the feast of Christmas, December 25, 1310.[51] That crown was made of thin iron in the form of laurel leaves, polished and shiny like a sword, and with many large pearls and other stones.

The emperor held a large and honorable court in Milan; and on the morning of January 1, 1311, the empress presented many gifts to his knights. He wanted to hear no mention of the Guelf or Ghibelline parties, but he was slandered by false reports: the Ghibellines said "he only wishes to see Guelfs," and the Guelfs said "he only receives Ghibellines;" and so each one feared the other. The Guelfs no longer went to see him; but the Ghibellines visited him often, because they had greater need of him. They thought that they deserved pride of place because they had suffered on behalf of the empire. But the emperor's will was very just, for he loved and honored each man like his own vassal.

The Cremonese went there to offer fealty in parliament with a clear conscience; the Genoese went to give him presents, and thanks to their love he

48. Filippone, count of Langasco and lord of Paria, was the father-in-law of Guidotto della Torre; though a Guelf, he favored coming to an agreement with Henry.

49. His son had married the daughter of Wenceslas IV, king of Bohemia.

50. The custom was to receive the crown of Italy at Milan (and not at Monza, as Compagni says here), the crown of Germany at Aachen, and the imperial crown at Rome.

51. The coronation actually took place on Epiphany, January 6, 1311.

ate from a golden plate at a great feast. Count Filippone resided at court; messer Manfredi di Beccheria, messer Antonio da Fisiraga, lord of Lodi, and other lords and barons of Lombardy appeared before the emperor. His life was not spent in song or hawking or amusements, but in endless meetings, appointing vicars for the cities and pacifying the contentious.

27 The Milanese had allocated money to be given to the emperor, and when the council met to raise this money, bitter words were exchanged by those from within the city and those returned from exile. Two sons of messer Guidotto began to regret what their father had done, and they paid heed to the complaints of their party. The emperor had the idea of taking some of the most powerful men of both parties and leading them away with him, and thus confine them.

The sons of messer Mosca, one of whom was archbishop, were cousins of messer Guidotto; they had become enemies through competition and so he held them in prison. The emperor made messer Guidotto free them and restored peace between them. But the sons of messer Guidotto did not keep the peace and one day they deliberately gathered their friends. Hatred was reawakened; in the council they exchanged insulting words which grew until they took arms and barricaded themselves in the houses of the della Torre. There was a tremendous uproar. The emperor's marshal went there with messer Galeazzo, son of messer Matteo Visconti; and messer Matteo went on foot with the emperor. The marshal charged the barricade with sixty mounted men and broke it and put the people to flight.

Though messer Guidotto was ill with gout, he was carried off to some other place; it was said that he escaped to the Dauphiné. His sons took refuge in one of their castles near Como, twenty miles from Milan. All their goods were plundered. And so ended the holiday, but not the emperor's affection: he wanted to pardon the della Torre, but they did not trust him. And then messer Matteo Visconti began to rise, and the della Torre and their friends to decline. Suspicion increased even more than hatred. The emperor entrusted the city to messer Matteo, and he left there as his vicar messer Niccolò Salimbeni of Siena, a wise and manly knight, adorned with good manners, magnanimous and generous with gifts.

28 The Enemy, who never sleeps but always sows and reaps, set discord in the hearts of the nobles of Cremona so they would rebel. Two brothers, sons of the marquis Cavalcabò, were lords there; and messer Sovramonte degli Amati, a wise knight, had almost become their enemy out of competition for offices. But they came to an agreement, moved by the letters and dishonest instigations of the Florentines. They raised a cry against the emperor and expelled his vicar.

The emperor did not fret when he heard this, but like a man of great spirit he summoned the rebels. They did not obey, and so broke faith and oath. The Florentines immediately sent an ambassador to make sure that the fire did not go out. He offered to help the Cremonese with men and money, which they accepted, and they reinforced the city.

The emperor rode towards Cremona. Ambassadors from Cremona fell at his feet, saying that they were poor men and could not support the burdens laid on them, and that they were willing to obey him without a vicar. The emperor did not reply, but they were informed by secret letters that if they wanted forgiveness, they should send many good citizens to ask for mercy since the emperor wanted to be honored. They sent plenty of them, barefoot and bareheaded, in simple tunics with leather collars around their necks; and they appeared before the emperor to ask for mercy. He did not speak to them, but kept riding towards the city while they kept asking for forgiveness. On arrival he found the gate open and entered. There he stopped, set hand to sword and drew it from its scabbard, and under the sword received the Cremonese. The great and powerful, who were at fault, and the noble Florentine knight messer Rinieri Buondelmonti, who was the podestà that had been sent to strengthen them against the emperor, all left before the emperor arrived. He seized all the powerful men who had remained, including messer Sovramonte, who thought himself too clever or too secure to flee. The emperor threw them in prison together with those who had come to ask for his mercy. He changed the government of the city, revoked his condemnation, and sent the prisoners to Romanengo.

29 While the emperor was residing in Cremona, the people of Brescia had obeyed his orders and received his vicar.[52] The leaders of the two parties there were messer Tebaldo Brusciati and messer Matteo di Maggio. Messer Matteo, who had ruled the city, obediently placed the government in the emperor's control; messer Tebaldo, who with his followers had wandered through Lombardy in poverty, was reestablished in his city by the emperor.

Messer Tebaldo, who had been given power by the emperor, betrayed

52. This paragraph is one of the rare places where I have not adhered closely to Compagni's text, which in this passage is extraordinarily compressed. By dividing Compagni's single sentence into several, and by incorporating a clause from the following paragraph, I have produced a rendering which is more lucid than the original.

him. When the emperor requested that some knights come serve him in Cremona, messer Tebaldo sent all those partisans of messer Matteo who had obeyed the emperor. When the emperor realized this, he sent for some others by name, and they did not come; he had them summoned, specifying deadlines and penalties, and still they did not come. The emperor understood their evil intentions. He left his chamber with a few companions, girded his sword, and turned his face towards Brescia; he put his hand to the sword, drew it half out of its scabbard, and cursed the city of Brescia. And he named a new vicar of Cremona.

On May 12, 1311, the emperor rode to Brescia with his troops and with a great part of the Lombards, including counts and lords. He laid siege to Brescia, because that is what he was advised to do. He was told that the city could not hold out because it was not stocked with provisions and the previous year's harvest was nearly exhausted. "And the people will surrender quickly when they see your camp pitched. But if you let Brescia go, all Lombardy is lost, for all your opponents will nest there. Let this be a victory to intimidate all the rest of them." He decided on the siege: he sent for master craftsmen, arranged buildings and tunnels and shelters, and openly prepared an assault. The city was very strong and inhabited by brave people; it had a fortress on the side towards the mountain, and the hill was sheer. The Brescians could not be denied access to that fortress, and the city was hard to attack. The emperor went forth one day with the idea of attacking the fortress from the side towards Germany, since if he could take it, the city would be conquered.

Messer Tebaldo went to try to succor the fortress; thanks to God's justice, his horse stumbled and fell. He was taken and led to the emperor, who rejoiced at his capture. The emperor tried messer Tebaldo and then had him dragged around the city on an ox hide; and finally he had his head cut off and his body quartered. And he had the other captives hanged.

The defenders likewise grew cruel towards those on the outside. When they captured one of them, they put him on the battlements where he could be seen, and there they flayed him and displayed great wickedness. And if any of the defenders were captured, they were hanged by the besiegers. And so those inside and outside the city warred fiercely on one another with towers and crossbows. Those outside were not able to press the siege so closely that spies sent by the Florentines could not enter the city, to encourage the Brescians with letters and bring them money.

One day messer Walerano, the emperor's brother and a handsome strapping fellow, rode around the city to take a look at it, wearing a vermilion jacket and with no helmet on his head. He was wounded in the neck by an arrow and died within a few days. They dressed him like a lord and carried him to Verona, where he was given an honorable burial. Many counts, knights, and barons, both Germans and Lombards, died there; and many fell ill, for the siege lasted until September 18.

The camp was in an awkward site and the heat was terrible; supplies had to be brought a great distance and the knights were not hardened warriors. Inside the city, many died of hunger and discomfort, for they had to stand guard and be very vigilant. Because of this, on September 19, 1311 an agreement was reached between the emperor and the Brescians, through the mediation of three cardinals—[Niccolò of Prato] the cardinal of Ostia, the cardinal of Albano, and messer Luca Fieschi—who had been sent to the emperor by the pope. The Brescians agreed to surrender the city with guarantees for their safety and that of their goods, and they put themselves in the hands of the cardinals.

The emperor entered the city, and he kept his agreement with them. He had the wall torn down and banished several Brescians. And he left the siege with far fewer knights than he had brought, for some died there and many went home ill.

30 The emperor left Brescia and went to Pavia because of a dispute that arose between the Beccheria and messer Riccardino, son of count Filippone. The bishop of Pavia had died, and each party wanted to select the new bishop. They disagreed so bitterly that the Beccheria faction killed four of their adversaries. The vicar and messer Riccardino battled the Beccheria faction until they expelled them from the city and stripped them of their castles outside it.

The emperor thought that he had lost enough time and so he rode towards Genoa, which was held by messer Branca d'Oria.[53] He arrived there on October 21, 1311 and messer Branca received him honorably and swore obedience.

Messer Obizzino Spinola, the leader of the other party and a rebel, went to meet the emperor and greeted him very reverently. The wise men deemed that it was the division between the two parties which earned the emperor his welcome, because the rivals competed in doing him honor. But the Genoese are by nature very haughty, proud, and quarrelsome with one another—so much so that old King Charles could never manage to unite them.

53. Actually, by Barnaba d'Oria.

They are so proud that no one believed that they would ever accept Henry as their lord, or even grant him passage. "The citizens are scornful, the terrain is harsh, the Germans take liberties with the ladies, the Genoese snarl at such behavior: there is sure to be a scuffle."

God, who rules and governs princes and peoples, tamed the Genoese. They restrained their wills, and like wise and noble men they honored Henry and hosted him in their city for several months. During that time death, which spares no one for long, by God's will took from the world the noble empress, minister to Christ's poor, who had a very noble reputation for the great sanctity of her good life. She was buried with great honor on November 12 in the main church of Genoa.[54]

31 The Florentines openly revealed themselves to be Henry's enemies by fomenting rebellion in the Lombard cities. They corrupted messer Giberto, lord of Parma, with money and written promises, and gave him fifteen thousand florins so that he would betray the emperor and incite the city to rise against him. Oh how much wickedness was undertaken by this knight, who had received from the emperor great favors in rapid succession! For the emperor had given him the fine castle of San Donnino and another noble castle on the banks of the Po, which he took from the Cremonese and gave to messer Giberto; and he had entrusted to his protection the fine city of Reggio, believing that he was a faithful and loyal knight. But messer Giberto took arms and cried "Death to the emperor" in the piazza of Parma; he expelled Henry's vicar from the city and welcomed his enemies. He cloaked his actions in false words, saying that he did this not for money but because Henry had reinstated in Cremona the marquis Pallavicino, whom he held to be his enemy.

The Florentines squeezed their poor citizens, taking their money and spending it on goods of this sort. They arranged to have messer Giberto reinstate the emperor's opponents in Cremona. He sustained them and reinforced their position on the banks of the Po, and one day he and perhaps a hundred horsemen in the service of the Brescians rode against messer Galeazzo, who was guarding Cremona. They entered the city, and so many sided with them that few remained faithful to the emperor—and those few had to leave the city.

Messer Guidotto della Torre rode to Cremona with knights gathered from Tuscany. They fortified the city with ditches and palisades. Count

54. Actually, December 14.

Filippone opposed the emperor fiercely; he sought to form a coalition, league, and marriage alliance with messer Giberto. The Brescian exiles joined them. But although the emperor in his mildness pardoned these men, God did not: the partisans of messer Tebaldo Brusciati, who had been pardoned by the emperor, wanted to take the city from the emperor once again; but the other faction received support more quickly and with weapons in hand chased them from Brescia and its countryside. Oh how greatly and quickly wickedness multiplied among the Lombards, as they killed each other and broke the oath they had given.

32 The Florentines who controlled Florence, filled with dread and fear, thought only of corrupting the lords of these places with promises and money. They extracted this money from their miserable citizens, who to preserve liberty let their money be taken little by little. They spent a lot of money on wicked works; their lives consisted of nothing but this sort of thing.

The *signori* chose secret messengers. Among them was a certain friar Bartolomeo, the son of a money changer, an astute man, familiar with England and well brought up in his youth, and of subtle intellect. They sent him to the Papal Court to bribe the pope and the cardinals. And they sent messer Baldo Fini of Figline with letters to bribe the king of France. The cardinal of Ostia [Niccolò of Prato] remarked to the king: "How impudent are these Florentines, who rush to bribe every lord with their ten flea eggs!"

They sent two ambassadors to the pope: messer Pino de' Rossi and messer Gherardo Bostichi, two worthy knights. A great deal of money was taken from them; they lost it, and did not get a thing they wanted from the pope.

Cardinal Pelagrù, a native of Gascony and nephew of the pope, was sent as legate to Bologna. The marquis of Ferrara had died and his bastard son ruled the city. And since he could not maintain his rule, he made a deal with the Venetians and sold Ferrara to them. The Venetians went there and occupied the city by force and ruled it. Messer Francesco d'Este, the brother of the marquis, formed an alliance with the Church together with the Bolognese and messer Orso degli Orsini of Rome. The cardinal went to Ferrara but the Venetians did not obey him. He therefore instituted a trial against them and condemned them: he announced a crusade against them, and many soldiers from a number of places attacked them to win the indulgence and the pay. The Venetians held a fortress in Ferrara which the marquis had made very strong, like a keep. The Venetians went to Ferrara by water and were defeated, and many of them were captured and killed. And it was their unfortunate luck that they lost so vilely, for the nobles who were there abandoned them.

Cardinal Pelagrú came to Florence and was received with the greatest honor. The war-carriage and knights went to meet him at the hospital of San Gallo. The religious went in procession to honor him, as did the great *popolani* of that party, on foot and horse.

He entered Florence. The Florentines took counsel with him frequently and informed him carefully about how they were negotiating with the pope so that he would delay the emperor's coming. They asked the cardinal to help in this, and he promised to do so. They gave him money, which he accepted willingly, and with it he paid for his legation. And he left Florence in concord with them.

The cardinal went to the emperor, who knew of his discussions with the Florentines and so did not show him much good will. He then returned to the pope, who encouraged him concerning the Florentine request and kept up their hopes in order to extract from them a great deal of money. And the Florentines did this in order that the emperor might wear himself out.

33 One of the three cardinals whom the pope had sent to the emperor at the siege of Brescia died. This was the cardinal of Albano, who arrived in Lucca ill and died there.

The bishop of Liège also died there. He was a dear friend of the emperor, who had given him Reggiolo, which is located between Reggio and Mantua. The Mantuans then took this town from the person left in charge of it.

The two Florentine ambassadors to the Papal Court died there. Messer Pino de' Rossi was first. As a reward for his labors, two of his relatives by blood and marriage were knighted by the *popolo* and given a lot of money, out of the funds taken from the Ghibellines and Whites. For even though the Whites retained a lingering loyalty to the Guelf Party, they were treated by it like mortal enemies. Then messer Gherardo died; and his relatives were honored with neither knighthood nor money, since he had not been as devoted as the other ambassador.

34 The Florentines, blinded by their presumption, behaved not like wise warriors, but like arrogant ones. They firmly opposed the emperor in league with the people of Bologna, Siena, Lucca, Volterra, Prato, Colle, and the other towns of their party. The Pistoiese, impoverished and exhausted, afflicted and devastated by war, did not align entirely with them—not because they were not of the same mind, but because they had been placed under a podestà with a salary so large that they could not support the expense. For this reason they would not have been able to pay their share of the levy, since they paid the marshal and his men forty-eight thousand florins a year; but they kept them, so that the Florentines would not enter their city.

The Lucchese always maintained ambassadors at the emperor's court; and sometimes they said that they would obey him if he would grant them letters saying they could keep the imperial lands which they held and if he would not reinstate the exiles. The emperor made no deal with them or with the others, but sent messer Luigi of Savoy and other ambassadors to Tuscany. They were honorably received by Lucca and given fine silk cloths and other presents. Prato and all the other cities gave them magnificent presents, and excuses for being in league with the Florentines.

Siena acted the whore: throughout this war it neither denied passage to the foes nor split entirely from the Florentines' will. The Bolognese sided firmly with the Florentines against the emperor, because they feared him greatly. They fortified themselves strongly and stockaded the city. It was said that they had no defense against him, because the Church had granted him passage; but because he thought that this would be a difficult route by which to enter Tuscany, he did not take it. And it was said that the Malispini marquises wanted to bring him through the Lunigiana, and they had prepared the roads and widened the narrow passes. If he had gone there, he would have fallen in with disloyal followers; but God guided him.

35 He left Genoa to go to Pisa, which was entirely of the imperial spirit and party. Pisa hoped for more from his advent than any other city. It sent him sixty thousand florins in Lombardy and promised him sixty thousand more once he was in Tuscany, thinking that it would regain its castles and lord it over its foes. Pisa is the city which gave him the rich sword as a mark of affection; which held festivals and celebrations for his successes; which received many threats on his account; which has always been an open gate for him and for the new lords who support that party, who have come to Tuscany by sea and by land; and which is carefully watched by the Florentines whenever they rejoice in the good fortunes of the Empire.

The emperor arrived in Pisa on March 6, 1312, with thirty galleys. He was received there with great festivities and joy, and honored as their lord. The Florentines sent no ambassadors there, because the citizens were not in accord. One moment they elected ambassadors to send to him, and then they did not send them; they placed more faith in simony and corrupting the court of Rome than in reaching an agreement with the emperor.

Messer Luigi of Savoy, the imperial ambassador to Tuscany, came to Florence and received little honor from the noble citizens, who did the opposite of what they should have done. He requested that they send an ambassador to honor the emperor and obey him as their lord. Messer Betto Brunelleschi answered on behalf of the *Signoria* that "the Florentines have never lowered their horns for any lord." And no ambassador was sent to the emperor, though they could have had very favorable terms from him, since the major impediment he faced was the Guelfs of Tuscany.

His ambassador left and returned to Pisa; and the Florentines had a siege tower built at Arezzo and resumed the war there. They showed themselves to be enemies of the emperor in every way, calling him a cruel tyrant and saying that he allied himself with the Ghibellines and did not want to see Guelfs. And in their decrees they proclaimed: "For the honor of the holy Church, and the death of the king of Germany." They removed the imperial eagles from their gates and from wherever else they were carved or painted, setting penalties for anyone who painted them or did not erase those already painted.

36 The emperor, derided by the Florentines, left Pisa and went to Rome. He arrived there on May 7, 1312, and was honorably received and given the position of senator. Because he recognized all the injuries done him by the Guelfs of Tuscany and found that the Ghibellines sided with him in good will, he changed his intentions and sided with the Ghibellines. He turned towards them the affection and benevolence which he had formerly held for the Guelfs. He decided to support them and to help restore them to their homes, and to consider the Guelfs and Blacks his enemies and persecute them.

The Florentines always kept ambassadors at the feet of King Robert, urging him to attack the emperor with his troops, promising and giving him plenty of money.

King Robert, like a wise lord and a friend of the Florentines, promised to help them, and he did so. But to the emperor he pretended that he was advising and admonishing the Florentines to obey him as their lord. When he heard that the emperor was in Rome, he immediately sent his brother messer Giovanni there with 300 mounted men, claiming that he had sent him to protect the emperor and honor his crown. But he really sent him to plot with the Orsini, enemies of the emperor, to corrupt the senate, and to impede the coronation. And the emperor was well aware of this.

The king, displaying great affection for the emperor, sent ambassadors to congratulate him on his arrival. They made grand offers, asking the emperor for a marriage alliance and saying that the king had sent his brother to honor his coronation and give him aid, if it were needed.

This wisest of emperors answered them from his own mouth: "The king's offers are slow in coming, and messer Giovanni is too swift." The imperial response was wise, for he understood very well the reason messer Giovanni had come.

On the first day of August 1312 Henry, count of Luxembourg, emperor, and king of the Romans, was crowned in Rome in the church of St. John Lateran by messer Niccolò, the cardinal from Prato, by messer Luca Fieschi, cardinal of Genoa, and by messer Arnaldo Pelagrú, cardinal of Gascony, by license and mandate of Pope Clement V and of his cardinals.[55]

37 How greatly does God's justice exalt his majesty, when with fresh miracles he shows humble folk that God does not forget their sufferings! When those who are oppressed by the powerful see that God remembers them, they find great peace of mind. And how openly is God's vengeance recognized after he has long delayed and suffered! For when he delays his judgment and many believe that it has slipped from his mind, he does this in order to punish all the more.

Among the Blacks, there were four leaders in this discord: messer Rosso della Tosa, messer Pazzino de' Pazzi, messer Betto Brunelleschi, and messer Geri Spini. Two more joined them later: messer Teghaio Frescobaldi and messer Gherardo Ventraia, a man of little faith.

These six knights constrained Folcieri, the podestà of Florence, to decapitate Masino Cavalcanti and one of the Gherardini. These men had the Priors named as they wished, and filled the other offices inside and outside the city. These men freed or condemned whoever they wished; they made the decisions and distributed favors and hardships as they wished.

38 Messer Rosso della Tosa was a knight of great spirit and the instigator of the discord among the Florentines, an enemy of the *popolo* and a

55. The actual date of the coronation was June 29; the same error was also made by Giovanni Villani. And the Arnaldo who participated in the coronation was not Cardinal Pelagrú, but Cardinal Arnaldo Fauger.

friend of tyrants. It was he who split the whole Guelf Party of Florence into Whites and Blacks. It was he who inflamed the citizens' discord. It was he who with his efforts, alliances, and promises kept the rest under his authority. He was very devoted to the Black Party and persecuted the Whites. In him the neighboring cities of the Black Party trusted, and with him they made agreements.

This man kept God waiting a long time, for he was more than seventy-five years old. He was walking one day when a dog ran between his feet and made him fall, so that he broke his knee. It became infected; and, martyred by the doctors, he died from the agony. He was buried with great honor, as befits a great citizen.

He left two sons, Simone and Gottifredi, who were knighted by the [Guelf] Party along with a young relative of theirs named Pinuccio, and they were given a lot of money. They were called the knights of the spinning wheel, since the money they were given had been taken from the poor little women who work the spinning wheels.

These two knights, his sons, wanted to live in great style and be honored, since they thought they deserved it for their father's sake. They began to decline, and messer Pino began to rise; and in a short time he made himself great.[56]

39 Messer Betto Brunelleschi and his house were of Ghibelline stock. He was rich in land and goods. He was infamous among the *popolo*, for in times of famine he locked up his grain and declared: "Either I get this price for it or it will never be sold." He treated the Whites and the Ghibellines very badly, for two reasons: first, so that he might be more trusted by those who ruled; second, because he could expect no mercy for having switched sides. He was often employed on embassies since he was a good orator. He was on familiar terms with Pope Boniface. When messer Napoleone Orsini was cardinal legate in Tuscany, he was thoroughly at home with him and held him in conversation, removing any hope of making peace between the Whites and Blacks of Florence.

This knight was largely responsible for the death of messer Corso Donati. Yet he was so thoroughly dedicated to evil that he did not care for God or the world; he discussed an agreement with the Donati, excusing himself and accusing others. One day while he was playing chess, two Donati youths and their companions came up to him in his house and wounded him many

56. Messer Pino was from another branch of the family.

times in the head, so badly that they left him for dead. But one of his sons
wounded a son of Bicicocco [Donati], who died within a few days. Messer
Betto survived for several days, so that it was thought he would live. But
some days later he died miserably, in a rage, without penitence or satisfac-
tion to God or the world, and with the great ill will of many citizens. Many
rejoiced at his death, for he was a terrible citizen.

40 Messer Pazzino de' Pazzi, one of the four principal leaders of the
city, sought peace with the Donati on his own behalf and that of messer Pino
de' Rossi—even though messer Pino bore little guilt for the death of messer
Corso, because he had been messer Corso's good friend and had cared for
little else. But the Cavalcanti, who were a powerful family and had about
sixty men who could bear arms, nursed a great hatred for these six leading
knights who had constrained Folcieri the podestà to decapitate Masino
Cavalcanti. They bore this without any open display.

One day Paffiera Cavalcanti, a very spirited young man, heard that
messer Pazzino had gone to the banks of the Arno near Santa Croce with a
falcon and just one servant. He mounted his horse with some companions
and they went to find him. When messer Pazzino saw them coming, he began to flee towards the Arno. Paffiera, pursuing him, struck him in the kid-
neys with a lance. He fell in the water, and they cut his veins and then fled
towards the Val di Sieve. And so he died miserably.

The Pazzi and Donati armed themselves and ran to the palace of the
Priors. They rushed to the Cavalcanti houses in the New Market with the
standard of justice and with part of the *popolo*, and with kindling they set
fire to three of the Cavalcanti palaces. Then they turned towards the house
of messer Brunetto, believing that he had instigated this deed.

Messer Ottaviano Cavalcanti was succored by the sons of messer Pino
and by his other friends. They made barricades and reinforced themselves
with mounted men and foot soldiers, so that nothing was done to them.
Inside the barricade were messer Gottifredi and messer Simone della Tosa,
Testa Tornaquinci and some of their kinsmen, some of the degli Scali, the
degli Agli, the Lucardesi, and many other families, who boldly defended the
Cavalcanti until they were constrained to lay down their arms.

Once the *popolo* had quieted down, the Pazzi brought charges against the
Cavalcanti, for which forty-eight of them were condemned in their goods
and their persons. Messer Ottaviano took refuge in a hospital, where the
Rossi guaranteed his safety. Then he went to Siena.

Messer Pazzino left many sons. Two of them were knighted by the *popolo*, along with two of their relatives, and they were given four thousand florins and forty measures of grain.

41 In how small a plot of ground, where justice is done and evildoers are punished with evil death, were five cruel citizens killed: messer Corso Donati, messer Nicola de' Cerchi, messer Pazzino de' Pazzi, Gherardo Bordoni, and Simone di messer Corso Donati.[57] Messer Rosso della Tosa and messer Betto Brunelleschi also died badly. And so they were punished for their sins.

Messer Geri Spini has been very wary ever since, for the Donati and their followers and the Bordoni—whose houses had been destroyed by the *popolo* not long before, to their great shame and harm—were welcomed home with great honor.

42 Such is our troubled city! Such are our citizens, obstinate in evildoing! And what is done one day is condemned the next. Wise men used to say: "A wise man does nothing which he regrets." In that city and among those citizens, there is no act so praiseworthy that it is not considered to be the opposite and blamed. There men kill one another and evil is not punished by the laws, for if the evildoer has friends and money to spend he is freed from the crime he committed.

Oh wicked citizens, who have corrupted and spoiled the whole world with bad practices and illicit profits! You are the ones who have brought every bad habit into the world. Now the world is beginning to turn against you: the emperor and his forces will seize and plunder you by sea and by land.[58]

---

57. In fact, these five deaths all occurred near the spot where criminals were executed.

58. When Compagni stopped writing in the summer of 1312, Henry was poised to attack Florence. But he retreated to San Casciano on October 31 and never resumed the enterprise. He died at Buonconvento, in the territory of Siena, on August 24, 1313.

INDEX OF
MODERN AUTHORS

INDEX

University of Pennsylvania Press

MIDDLE AGES SERIES

Edward Peters, General Editor

F. R. P. Akehurst, trans. *The* Coutumes de Beauvaisis *of Philippe de Beaumanoir*. 1992

Peter L. Allen. *The Art of Love: Amatory Fiction from Ovid to the* Romance of the Rose. 1992

David Anderson. *Before the Knight's Tale: Imitation of Classical Epic in Boccaccio's* Teseida. 1988

Benjamin Arnold. *Count and Bishop in Medieval Germany: A Study of Regional Power, 1100–1350*. 1991

Mark C. Bartusis. *The Late Byzantine Army: Arms and Society, 1204–1453*. 1992

Thomas N. Bisson, ed. *Cultures of Power: Lordship, Status, and Process in Twelfth-Century Europe*. 1995

Uta-Renate Blumenthal. *The Investiture Controversy: Church and Monarchy from the Ninth to the Twelfth Century*. 1988

Gerald A. Bond. *The Loving Subject: Desire, Eloquence, and Power in Romanesque France*. 1995

Daniel Bornstein, trans. *Dino Compagni's* Chronicle of Florence. 1986

Maureen Boulton. *The Song in the Story: Lyric Insertions in French Narrative Fiction, 1200–1400*. 1993

Betsy Bowden. *Chaucer Aloud: The Varieties of Textual Interpretation*. 1987

Charles R. Bowlus. *Franks, Moravians, and Magyars: The Struggle for the Middle Danube, 788–907*. 1995

James William Brodman. *Ransoming Captives in Crusader Spain: The Order of Merced on the Christian-Islamic Frontier*. 1986

Kevin Brownlee and Sylvia Huot, eds. *Rethinking the* Romance of the Rose: *Text, Image, Reception*. 1992

Matilda Tomaryn Bruckner. *Shaping Romance: Interpretation, Truth, and Closure in Twelfth-Century French Fictions*. 1993

Otto Brunner (Howard Kaminsky and James Van Horn Melton, eds. and trans.). Land *and Lordship: Structures of Governance in Medieval Austria.* 1992

Robert I. Burns, S.J., ed. *Emperor of Culture: Alfonso X the Learned of Castile and His Thirteenth-Century Renaissance.* 1990

David Burr. *Olivi and Franciscan Poverty: The Origins of the* Usus Pauper *Controversy.* 1989

David Burr. *Olivi's Peaceable Kingdom: A Reading of the Apocalypse Commentary.* 1993

Thomas Cable. *The English Alliterative Tradition.* 1991

Anthony K. Cassell and Victoria Kirkham, eds. and trans. *Diana's Hunt/Caccia di Diana: Boccaccio's First Fiction.* 1991

John C. Cavadini. *The Last Christology of the West: Adoptionism in Spain and Gaul, 785–820.* 1993

Brigitte Cazelles. *The Lady as Saint: A Collection of French Hagiographic Romances of the Thirteenth Century.* 1991

Karen Cherewatuk and Ulrike Wiethaus, eds. *Dear Sister: Medieval Women and the Epistolary Genre.* 1993

Anne L. Clark. *Elisabeth of Schönau: A Twelfth-Century Visionary.* 1992

Willene B. Clark and Meradith T. McMunn, eds. *Beasts and Birds of the Middle Ages: The Bestiary and Its Legacy.* 1989

Richard C. Dales. *The Scientific Achievement of the Middle Ages.* 1973

Charles T. Davis. *Dante's Italy and Other Essays.* 1984

William J. Dohar. *The Black Death and Pastoral Leadership: The Diocese of Hereford in the Fourteenth Century.* 1994

Katherine Fischer Drew, trans. *The Burgundian Code.* 1972

Katherine Fischer Drew, trans. *The Laws of the Salian Franks.* 1991

Katherine Fischer Drew, trans. *The Lombard Laws.* 1973

Nancy Edwards. *The Archaeology of Early Medieval Ireland.* 1990

Richard K. Emmerson and Ronald B. Herzman. *The Apocalyptic Imagination in Medieval Literature.* 1992

Theodore Evergates. *Feudal Society in Medieval France: Documents from the County of Champagne.* 1993

Felipe Fernández-Armesto. *Before Columbus: Exploration and Colonization from the Mediterranean to the Atlantic, 1229–1492.* 1987

Jerold C. Frakes. *Brides and Doom: Gender, Property, and Power in Medieval Women's Epic.* 1994

R. D. Fulk. *A History of Old English Meter.* 1992

Patrick J. Geary. *Aristocracy in Provence: The Rhône Basin at the Dawn of the Carolingian Age.* 1985

Peter Heath. *Allegory and Philosophy in Avicenna (Ibn Sînâ), with a Translation of the Book of the Prophet Muḥammad's Ascent to Heaven.* 1992

J. N. Hillgarth, ed. *Christianity and Paganism, 350–750: The Conversion of Western Europe.* 1986

Richard C. Hoffmann. *Land, Liberties, and Lordship in a Late Medieval Countryside: Agrarian Structures and Change in the Duchy of Wrocław.* 1990

Robert Hollander. *Boccaccio's Last Fiction:* Il Corbaccio. 1988

John Y. B. Hood. *Aquinas and the Jews.* 1995

Edward B. Irving, Jr. *Rereading* Beowulf. 1989

Richard A. Jackson, ed. Ordines Coronationis Franciae: *Texts and Ordines for the Coronation of Frankish and French Kings and Queens in the Middle Ages, Vol. I.* 1995

C. Stephen Jaeger. *The Envy of Angels: Cathedral Schools and Social Ideals in Medieval Europe, 950–1200.* 1994

C. Stephen Jaeger. *The Origins of Courtliness: Civilizing Trends and the Formation of Courtly Ideals, 939–1210.* 1985

Donald J. Kagay, trans. *The Usatges of Barcelona: The Fundamental Law of Catalonia.* 1994

Richard Kay. *Dante's Christian Astrology.* 1994

Ellen E. Kittell. *From* Ad Hoc *to* Routine: *A Case Study in Medieval Bureaucracy.* 1991

Alan C. Kors and Edward Peters, eds. *Witchcraft in Europe, 1100–1700: A Documentary History.* 1972

Barbara M. Kreutz. *Before the Normans: Southern Italy in the Ninth and Tenth Centuries.* 1992

Michael P. Kuczynski. *Prophetic Song: The Psalms as Moral Discourse in Late Medieval England.* 1995

E. Ann Matter. *The Voice of My Beloved: The Song of Songs in Western Medieval Christianity.* 1990

Shannon McSheffrey. *Gender and Heresey: Women and Men in Lollard Communities, 1420–1530.* 1995

A. J. Minnis. *Medieval Theory of Authorship.* 1988

Lawrence Nees. *A Tainted Mantle: Hercules and the Classical Tradition at the Carolingian Court.* 1991

Lynn H. Nelson, trans. *The Chronicle of San Juan de la Peña: A Fourteenth-Century Official History of the Crown of Aragon.* 1991

Barbara Newman. *From Virile Woman to WomanChrist: Studies in Medieval Religion and Literature.* 1995

Joseph F. O'Callaghan. *The Learned King: The Reign of Alfonso X of Castile.* 1993

Odo of Tournai (Irven M. Resnick, trans.). *Two Theological Treatises:* On Original Sin *and* A Disputation with the Jew, Leo, Concerning the Advent of Christ, the Son of God. 1994

David M. Olster. *Roman Defeat, Christian Response, and the Literary Construction of the Jew.* 1994

William D. Paden, ed. *The Voice of the Trobairitz: Perspectives on the Women Troubadours.* 1989

Edward Peters. *The Magician, the Witch, and the Law.* 1982

Edward Peters, ed. *Christian Society and the Crusades, 1198–1229: Sources in Translation, including* The Capture of Damietta *by Oliver of Paderborn.* 1971

Edward Peters, ed. *The First Crusade: The* Chronicle of Fulcher of Chartres *and Other Source Materials.* 1971

Edward Peters, ed. *Heresy and Authority in Medieval Europe.* 1980

James M. Powell. *Albertanus of Brescia: The Pursuit of Happiness in the Early Thirteenth Century.* 1992

James M. Powell. *Anatomy of a Crusade, 1213–1221.* 1986

Susan A. Rabe. *Faith, Art, and Politics at Saint-Riquier: The Symbolic Vision of Angilbert.* 1995

Jean Renart (Patricia Terry and Nancy Vine Durling, trans.). *The Romance of the Rose or Guillaume de Dole.* 1993

Michael Resler, trans. Erec *by Hartmann von Aue.* 1987

Pierre Riché (Michael Idomir Allen, trans.). *The Carolingians: A Family Who Forged Europe.* 1993

Pierre Riché (Jo Ann McNamara, trans.). *Daily Life in the World of Charlemagne.* 1978

Jonathan Riley-Smith. *The First Crusade and the Idea of Crusading.* 1986

Joel T. Rosenthal. *Patriarchy and Families of Privilege in Fifteenth-Century England.* 1991

Teofilo F. Ruiz. *Crisis and Continuity: Land and Town in Late Medieval Castile.* 1994

James A. Rushing, Jr. *Images of Adventure: Ywain in the Visual Arts.* 1995

James A. Schultz. *The Knowledge of Childhood in the German Middle Ages, 1100–1350.* 1995

Pamela Sheingorn, ed. and trans. *The Book of Sainte Foy.* 1995

Robin Chapman Stacey. *The Road to Judgment: From Custom to Court in Medieval Ireland and Wales.* 1994

Sarah Stanbury. *Seeing the* Gawain-*Poet: Description and the Act of Perception.* 1992

Robert D. Stevick. *The Earliest Irish and English Bookarts: Visual and Poetic Forms Before A.D. 1000.* 1994

Thomas C. Stillinger. *The Song of Troilus: Lyric Authority in the Medieval Book.* 1992

Susan Mosher Stuard. *A State of Deference: Ragusa/Dubrovnik in the Medieval Centuries.* 1992

Susan Mosher Stuard, ed. *Women in Medieval History and Historiography.* 1987

Susan Mosher Stuard, ed. *Women in Medieval Society.* 1976

Jonathan Sumption. *The Hundred Years War: Trial by Battle.* 1992

Ronald E. Surtz. *The Guitar of God: Gender, Power, and Authority in the Visionary World of Mother Juana de la Cruz (1451–1534).* 1990

Ronald E. Surtz. *Writing Women in Late Medieval and Early Modern Spain: The Mothers of Saint Teresa of Avila.* 1995

Del Sweeney, ed. *Agriculture in the Middle Ages.* 1995

William H. TeBrake. *A Plague of Insurrection: Popular Politics and Peasant Revolt in Flanders, 1323–1328.* 1993

Patricia Terry, trans. *Poems of the Elder Edda.* 1990

Hugh M. Thomas. *Vassals, Heiresses, Crusaders, and Thugs: The Gentry of Angevin Yorkshire, 1154–1216.* 1993

Mary F. Wack. *Lovesickness in the Middle Ages: The* Viaticum *and Its Commentaries.* 1990

Benedicta Ward. *Miracles and the Medieval Mind: Theory, Record, and Event, 1000–1215.* 1982

Suzanne Fonay Wemple. *Women in Frankish Society: Marriage and the Cloister, 500–900.* 1981

Kenneth Baxter Wolf. *Making History: The Normans and Their Historians in Eleventh-Century Italy.* 1995

Jan M. Ziolkowski. *Talking Animals: Medieval Latin Beast Poetry, 750–1150.* 1993